DIVINE EMBLEMS

A.B. SIMPSON

DIVINE EMBLEMS

*Practical
lessons from
Old Testament
symbolism*

Christian Publications
Camp Hill, Pennsylvania

Christian Publications
3825 Hartzdale Drive, Camp Hill, PA 17011

Faithful, biblical publishing since 1883

ISBN: 0-87509-588-7
LOC Catalog Card Number: 94-72913
© 1995 by Christian Publications
All rights reserved
Printed in the United States of America

95 96 97 98 99 5 4 3 2 1

Cover Photograph © 1995 by David Monyer

CONTENTS

CHAPTER 1

Emblems from the Story of Creation

While the Holy Scriptures are a literal and historical record of things that have actually occurred, underlying the narrative there is a deeper spiritual meaning. Using the province of faith, under the teaching of the Holy Spirit, it is up to us reverently to interpret and apply. While there is danger of excess and extravagance in this direction, this must not drive us to the opposite extreme of hard and cold literalism. The Holy Scriptures have given us the true principle of such spiritual interpretation, and there we learn both by divine statement and innumerable examples that "these things happened . . . as examples and were written down as warnings for us, on whom the fulfillment of the ages has come" (1 Corinthians 10:11). These underlying spiritual teachings are not confined to those things which may be strictly termed types, but in a measure are linked with all the events of the sacred record.

In the following chapters and reflections I will not attempt to elaborate any rigid or complete system of typology. Rather, I will, with simplicity and freedom, endeavor to draw the most practical and spiritual lessons, enabled by the divine Spirit, from the leading types and events of inspired record which have more or less precisely a symbolic character and scriptural suggestiveness.

The Creation

The first is the story of the creation. Recognizing, of course, the literal and historical reality of the record, we have the authority of the Scriptures themselves to regard it as the figure of the new creation. The divine Spirit is working this out in the hearts of God's people, and ultimately will consummate in the kingdom of glory. "For we are God's workmanship, created in Christ Jesus to do good works, which God prepared in advance for us to do" (Ephesians 2:10). "Therefore, if anyone is in Christ, he is a new creation; the old has gone, the new has come!" (2 Corinthians 5:17).

The first chapter of Genesis is repeated in the twenty-first chapter of Revelation, "Then I saw a new heaven and a new earth, for the first heaven and the first earth had passed away" (21:1). Underlying the whole record of the first creation we can trace the story of grace in figure and spiritual foreshadowing. Like that ancient process, the new creation begins in wreck and chaos—a wreck like that of primeval order. The new creation, like the old, emerges from a scene of darkness and desolation. Like that also, it is preceded and introduced by the overshadowing presence and brooding wings of the heavenly Dove, and brought about by the power of the personal and Almighty Word. Then, also, the first type of Christ in both creations is the dawning Light. "For God, who said, 'Let light shine out of darkness,' made his light shine in our hearts to give us the light of the knowledge of the glory of God in the face of Christ" (2 Corinthians 4:6). Light is followed by order and the separation of the things that differ, and this word *separation* is almost a keynote of the entire spiritual life and has a radical reference to the principle of sanctification itself.

In the old creation there was much light before the celestial luminaries appeared in the firmament. That was not until the fourth day. So in the spiritual life the manifestation of Jesus in His personal indwelling and glory comes often at a later stage. Perhaps the three days that preceded it in the creation narrative suggest, if they do not typify, the resurrection experience which must ever precede it. Salvation brings us the light of the Holy Spirit, but our deeper consecration and union with Him introduces us to the full glory of the Sun of Righteousness and to the dawn of that day whose "sun will no more be your light by day . . . for the LORD will be your everlasting light, and your God will be your glory" (Isaiah 60:19). This is followed in the old creation by the introduction, in all its wonderful forms and fullness, of life in the entire animal kingdom. And so in the new creation, the revelation of the indwelling Christ quickens into life the whole spiritual being and fills it in every part with fruitfulness and fullness of life, until it reaches its climax in the new man in his full maturity, reflecting the glorious image of God Himself.

In both the old creation and the new there were successive stages with marked intervals like the great strata of our globe, bearing the traces of intense convulsions and mighty upheavals. So, too, with the transformation in our spiritual life, God has to break off from the old experiences and bring us out into new aspirations and higher planes by forces often as convulsive as those which molded earth's earlier ages.

And in each case it will be noticed in the records of Genesis that the progress is from the lower to the higher, from the darker to the brighter, from the evening to the morning.

Every new stage begins in comparative evening and ends in a clear morning, and it is as true now as in the creation days, "and there was evening, and there was morning—the first day" (Genesis 1:5). So the transformation is going forward in every Christian heart, and "the path of the righteous is like the first gleam of dawn, shining ever brighter till the full light of day" (Proverbs 4:18). So, too, the kingdom of God is going forward through the ages of time, and by and by it will be evening and morning, one eternal day.

"He who was seated on the throne said, 'I am making everything new!' " (Revelation 21:5).

The Creation of Man

The crown of the first creation was man himself. The story of his formation is accompanied with greater emphasis and fullness of detail than the entire universe. It was determined in the counsels of the eternal Trinity, "Let us make man"—he was patterned after nothing less than the Creator Himself—"in our image" and "in our likeness" (Genesis 1:26).

It is fitting that such a majestic being should be the sovereign of the lower creation, and therefore he was invested with the lordship of nature, "Rule over the fish of the sea and the birds of the air and over every living creature that moves on the ground" (1:28). It was natural, therefore, that if the material creation is symbolic of redemption, much more is the creation of man the type of the Holy Spirit's chief work of grace, namely the renewal and restoration of the human soul. Hence, we find in the New Testament epistles such language as this: "Put on the new self, created to be like God in true righteousness and holiness" (Ephesians 4:24). "Put on the new self, which is being renewed in knowledge in the image of its Creator" (Colossians 3:10). "If anyone is in Christ, he is a new creation; the old has gone, the new has come!" (2 Corinthians 5:17).

As before, so here we find many exquisite points of correspondence and resemblance. The natural man was created by the forming hand and breathing breath of his Maker; so the spiritual man is not only externally reformed, but internally renewed and regenerated by the very breath and Spirit of the living God. "The LORD God . . . breathed into his nostrils the breath of life, and the man became a living being" (Genesis 2:7). The Holy Spirit breathes into us the spirit of life, and the new man becomes a quickened spirit. "So it is written: 'The first man Adam became a living being'; the last Adam, a life-giving spirit" (1 Corinthians 15:45). "And just as we have borne the likeness of the earthly man, so shall we bear the likeness of the man from heaven" (15:49).

Again, the first man was created in the likeness of God. Likewise the new creation reaches forward to this glorious ideal, namely, "to be conformed to the likeness of his Son" (Romans 8:29). "Both the one who makes men holy and those who are made holy are of the same family. So Jesus is not ashamed to call them brothers" (Hebrews 2:11). "But we know that when he appears, we shall be like him, for we shall see him as he is" (1 John 3:2).

Further, the old creation invested man with kingliness and lordship; so the new creation makes us kings and priests unto God. Its consummation will be reached when in the millennial world we will reign with Christ over the material earth, and the picture of the eighth Psalm will be totally fulfilled: He has "put everything under his feet" (8:6).

Man must first regain his lost dominion in the kingdom of his own heart. Then he will receive again the crown of nature and the lordship of creation, when he is prepared to administer it with the righteousness and beneficence of a perfect nature, a divine wisdom, and holiness.

There is a still higher emblem in the creation of man which the Apostle Paul has developed with great power and beauty in Romans and Corinthians. That is the relation that Adam sustains to the Lord Jesus Christ as the type of His Headship for redeemed humanity. Adam was created not merely as an isolated individual, but as the father and representative of the entire race, and his fall has involved his entire posterity in its bitter and baneful consequences. In like manner the Lord Jesus, the second Adam, stands not for Himself alone as an isolated individual, but as the representative of His entire people, for whom His suffering and death are accepted as an atoning sacrifice and a complete expiation, and His holy obedience as their imputed righteousness and the ground of their complete justification before God. Therefore we read in the passages already referred to, "For just as through the disobedience of the one man the many were made sinners, so also through the obedience of the one man the many will be made righteous" (Romans 5:19). "Just as the result of one trespass was condemnation for all men, so also the result of one act of righteousness was justification that brings life for all men" (5:18). "For as in Adam all die, so in

Christ all will be made alive" (1 Corinthians 15:22).

The extent of Christ's representation is as universal, in the real principle, as Adam's. Adam's headship and its painful consequences extend to all his posterity. Christ's headship and its glorious blessings extend to all His spiritual posterity; that is, all and only those who are born of Him. Therefore the whole human race will not be saved, but the whole Christ race will. And the new birth is the indispensable condition and the vital link between Christ and His constituents. The true reading of the passage already quoted in First Corinthians 15, is in beautiful accord with this teaching. "For as all who are in Adam die, so all who are in Christ will be made alive." The great question, therefore, for each one of us, is: have we passed out of the Adam life into the Christ life? Salvation, consequently, is not in any sense a culture or improvement of our natural life, but it is the renunciation and crucifixion, not only of the sin, but of the self. The entire nature must die, and all who will live forever must be born of Christ, who comes down from heaven through the Holy Spirit into our hearts and lives. Salvation, therefore, is a radical and inexorable death sentence upon the flesh, both in its grosser and higher parts, and a supernatural and divine creation, more wonderful than the birth of the universe, and equivalent to the resurrection of the dead. Stupendous fact! God's mightiest handwork! Have you experienced it, and can you say, "the new has come!" (2 Corinthians 5:17)?

The Creation of Woman

The story of the birth of Eve is more exquisitely beautiful than any dream of ancient poetry or conception of art or imagination. The nearest approach to it is Socrates' celebrated description in Greek literature. He represented the human form as originally double, facing both ways, and afterwards divided by the gods into the sexes, so that every man and woman forms but a half of his or her former self, which is constantly searching for its counterpart. But this is clumsy and coarse compared with the sacred idyll of woman's lovely birth, which represents her as originally in the man, and then gently taken out of him while he slept, created into beauty and fitness for his fellowship, and then given back to him as his partner and helpmate for life.

The exquisite signification of this in connection with the human and social relation of man and woman—the tender unity, the perfect equality, the mutual independence and the sacred affection which should ever link them together—does not belong to our present theme. But its spiritual beauty and teaching are even finer and more wonderful, for we have here the parable of the Lord Jesus Christ Himself, and His relations to the Church, His heavenly Bride, which really contains the germ of the entire mystery of redemption.

First, we see Eve in her original creation in

Adam; so the Church was in Christ. Adam was not only an individual man, but rather man in the general sense, containing in himself in his original formation the woman as well as the man. So the Lord Jesus was not only one of the sons of men, but the Son of man, humanity summed up in one complete personality, containing in Himself the germ and substance of all the spiritual lives that are to be born of Him. Therefore we are identified really with Him, and so His life and death, His sufferings and obedience are actually ours, for us as well as for Him.

Second, Eve was taken out of Adam while he slept and really formed of his physical substance; so while Jesus slept in the sepulcher in death the Church was born out of His substance, and every believer is created anew in Christ Jesus. Our life is part of His very being. We are "partakers of the divine nature" (2 Peter 1:4, KJV). Christ is actually formed in us, and we are part of His resurrection life as truly as Eve was of Adam's. We are described as "risen with Christ" (Colossians 3:1, KJV), and our "life is now hidden with Christ in God" (3:3). Christ is our life. This is the great mystery of the spiritual life; it is a miracle of life; it is not mere life, but Christ life.

The Hebrew expression which describes the formation of Eve is the word "builded." He builded the rib into the woman. How perfectly it describes the whole process of the completion of the body of Christ. The same word is used by the apostle in describing it: "In him you too are being built together to become a dwelling in which God lives by his Spirit" (Ephesians 2:22). The language of Adam to his partner, "This is now bone of my bones and flesh of my flesh" (Genesis 2:23), was literally true, but just as strikingly true is it now that "we are members of his body, of his flesh, and of his bones" (Ephesians 5:30, KJV).

Third, Eve was given back to Adam to be his partner and bride and a helpmate for him. Her very life by its origin and intention was for him, and not for herself; therefore woman by her very constitution is made not for selfishness, but for service and love. She finds her true destiny in living for man, and losing her life and personality in the one she loves. So the soul born of Christ belongs to Christ; so the Church taken out of His life is given back to Him as the Bride of His love and partner of His throne. The soul born of God must rise to God and live for God, and every impulse and element of its spiritual life and consecration finds its rest in losing itself in God and living only for His glory.

This wonderful truth runs like a bridal wreath all through the Holy Scriptures. We see it not only in the marriage of Eden, but in the wedding of Rebekah, in the love of Jacob and Rachel, in Solomon's song, in the vision of Hosea, in the marriage feast of Canaan, in the parable of the Ten Virgins, in the strange figurative language Paul has used of Christ and the Church, and finally in the majestic vision of the marriage supper of the Lamb. Not only is it true of the

Church as a whole, but it must naturally be just as real in the experience of all who are members of that mystical body. Of each of us, as individuals, He says: "Your Maker is your husband" (Isaiah 54:5). "You will call me 'my husband'" (Hosea 2:16). "Listen, O daughter, consider and give ear: Forget your people and your father's house. The king is enthralled by your beauty; honor him, for he is your lord" (Psalm 45:10-11). "The body is . . . for the Lord, and the Lord for the body" (1 Corinthians 6:13). "We are members of his body, of his flesh, and of his bones" (Ephesians 5:30, KJV). Have we learned this holy, tender, ineffable secret of the Lord and of the heart, and within the chambers of His presence has it been true of us:

> Precious, gentle, lovely Jesus,
>   Blessed Bridegroom of my heart,
> In Thy secret inner chambers,
>   Thou hast whispered what Thou art.

The Sabbath

The creation of the world and the family is followed by the appointment of the Sabbath, which, with the home, forms the only relic left to man of Eden. While undoubtedly intended to be literally understood and observed as a day of holy rest, and while the creation is really the basis of all subsequent legislation regarding this day, and even the Mosaic institution was but a reenactment of the Sabbath of creation, and the words of

Christ concerning it look back to the very beginning—while all this is literally true and can never
be set aside by the passing away of Judaism, yet
below and beyond the natural day and its obligations there lies a deep spiritual symbolism. In the
fourth chapter of Hebrews Paul implies that it is
designed to be the figure of the deeper spiritual
rest into which He would lead His people. The
source and nature of this rest are finely expressed
by the words suggested by the meaning of the
day: "For anyone who enters God's rest also rests
from his own work, just as God did from his"
(Hebrews 4:10). It is the true secret of entering
Christ's rest. Struggling for our own righteousness, striving for our own will, will never bring it.
"Come to me, all you who are weary and burdened," is His cry, "and I will give you rest"
(Matthew 11:28). When we cease from our attempts to justify ourselves and accept His
righteousness, we have the rest of pardon. When
we cease from our attempts to sanctify ourselves
and accept His indwelling life and holiness, we
have the rest of holiness. When we cease from
our self-will and accept His will and take His
yoke upon us, we have the peace of God that passes all understanding. Evermore will it be true:

I struggled and wrestled to win it,
   The blessing that setteth me free,
But when I had ceased from my struggling,
   His peace Jesus gave unto me.

It is very remarkable and beautiful that although, until Christ's resurrection, the Sabbath was the seventh day of the week, it was actually the first full day of Adam's life. The first sun that ever rose on his vision was the Sabbath sun. Because he was created on the evening of the sixth day, Adam's first Sabbath was in this respect the foreshadowing of the Christian Sabbath (the first day of the week). The beautiful teaching of this fact is that we need to begin with rest, and not wait to end with it. We are not fitted for service until we are rested first with God's peace.

Christ will not lay His burden on an overloaded heart any more than a humane person would overload a weary beast of burden. Therefore the Christian Sabbath begins the week, teaching us that we must enter into rest before we are prepared for any service. The heaven that most people are looking for when they die should come as soon as they begin to live and prepare them for all life's labors and burdens. Therefore our dear Lord has said, "Come to me," first, and "I will give you rest." Then "take my yoke upon you" (11:29), and "with rested hearts go forth to serve Me." Have we entered into His rest—His glorious rest? Have we not only the peace, but the "perfect peace" in which He will keep the heart that is stayed on Him (Isaiah 26:3)? Oh, let us listen to the calm voice that comes down to us from that sweet Eden morning, and from that other garden and morning by Joseph's empty tomb, where restlessness and weariness find repose in His rest and all sufficiency.

Over an English cathedral door, on the Isle of Wight, rests a marble figure of a woman lying with her beautiful head on a Bible open at the words, "Come unto me, all ye that labour and are heavy laden, and I will give you rest." It is the memorial of a royal princess who languished for years in the prison, and at last was found one morning with her lovely head resting on that verse and the tears still moist upon the page. Her weariness had found its pillow on His breast. So let us rest, before the icy hand of death stills our throbbing pulses, and leaning there on His strength find:

His fullness lies around our incompleteness,
Round our restlessness His rest.

The Garden

In the Hebrew, the word Eden signifies "delight," and the word garden has passed into the term "paradise," which represents an enclosure of natural beauty and culture, combining exquisiteness of scenery and all the delights of climate and production which natural conditions can secure. It was not intended as a scene of indolence and sensual delight, but as a congenial home, and a scene of occupation and service for a holy and happy race. God always meant His intelligent creatures to be employed, and heaven will be a scene of active and continual service.

This primeval paradise stands as a symbol of

our future home and is reproduced with higher conditions of felicity and glory in the closing chapter of Revelation, the vision of the future state of the glorified. That it will be a scene of delight in the physical beauty and perfection of the millennial earth and the new earth and heaven, there can be no question. Not forever will the soil of earth bring forth its piercing thorns and poison plants, rugged rocks and barren wastes. The blood of Calvary has redeemed and brought back an inheritance, infinitely more than Adam lost. "Instead of the thornbush will grow the pine tree, and instead of briers the myrtle will grow" (55:13). "You will go out in joy and be led forth in peace; the mountains and hills will burst into song before you, and all the trees of the field will clap their hands" (55:12). Man's highest dream of beauty and God's divine ideal of blessing will be fully realized, and earth will smile in all the loveliness of paradise restored. Let us therefore look upon the picture and hasten its realization by laboring and praying for His coming. Without Him earth can never become a paradise again.

The figure of the garden is strangely linked with all the scenes of redemption. Not only does it recall the happy memories of Eden and the sad story of the Fall, but it was in a garden that the tides of sin and judgment were rolled back by a suffering Redeemer, when with agony unutterable and sweat-like drops of blood He canceled our sins in Gethsemane and planted in the garden of our life by those blood drops the seed of hope and promise. It was in a garden, too, that He was buried and that the seed of His own precious body was planted as a kernel of wheat which fell into the ground to die according to His own sublime figure. And it was in a garden that He rose again; it was forth from the spring blossoms and vernal sunshine of that Easter morning that the seed of promise sprang into immortal life and light, and the hopes of our salvation and glory emerged in the resurrection life of Jesus.

The garden of Gethsemane and the garden of Joseph have undone the wrong of the garden of the Fall, and opened the gates of Eden and its innocence and happiness again. So the figure of the garden is carried in the rich symbolism of the prophets and poets of the Bible into the region of our spiritual life. "A garden locked up . . . an orchard of pomegranates" (Song of Songs 4:12-13), and precious fruits and heavenly flowers, is the metaphor by which the Master describes His work of grace in the consecrated heart. The graces of the Christian life are exhibited under the figure of all the fruits of nature. The care of the husbandman is illustrated by the methods and forms of human culture, and even the rivers of Eden become a suggestion, if not a symbol, of the streams of grace which make glad the City of God. The crown of the restored earth and the glorified heaven is the last garden of the divine panorama. There all the blessedness will be more than restored. The river of the water of life will flow through its midst from the very throne of God and the Lamb. All trees of beauty and fruitfulness will cover its banks and yield fruit not only according to the seasons of earth, but every month, in a perpetual fullness and fruitfulness of life and delight. There will be no more curse, nor night, nor death, nor even the occasional visitation of God, for it will be His personal abode and the metropolis of all creation. The tabernacle of God will be with men, and earth and heaven will be the eternal home of Christ and His redeemed. The scene of blessedness will be such as our highest thought cannot even conceive.

The Tree of Life

This is described in literal terms as one of the actual productions of the garden. It was in the midst of the garden, and perhaps was its crowning production and glory. It is evident that it was the means of sustaining and perpetuating the physical life of man, for after the Fall it was withdrawn from his reach for the express reason that it was not then fitting with his fallen nature that he should still partake of it and thus live forever. A perpetual physical life in his new condition would not only be contrary to the curse already pronounced, but would itself be a curse to him. It is therefore plain that even in Eden his physical life was not self-sustaining, but dependent upon supplies from sources beyond himself. Was it not designated thus to teach us that our physical life is not self-constituted, but needs to be divinely sustained? If the tree of life is a type of Jesus Christ, if He is the Source and Center of all life to fallen man, then the lesson is most emphatic and blessed that He is to us the Source of our physical as well as our spiritual strength and well-being. Did He not teach this expressly in His own words in the temptation: "Man does not live on bread alone, but on every word that comes from the mouth of God" (Matthew 4:4); and still more clearly and vividly in His discourse concerning the living bread, "the one who feeds on me will live because of me" (John 6:57); "Whoever eats my flesh and drinks my blood remains in me, and I in him" (6:56)?

It may be objected that the tree of life was withdrawn after the Fall, and that this teaches us that we have no right to look for supernatural physical strength on account of our fallen state and moral curse. But in the revelation of mercy made after the Fall, we are told, in language which I will more fully expound on in the next chapter, that God placed at the gate of the garden cherubim "to guard the way to the tree of life" (Genesis 3:24) Notice it was not to close the way, but to keep the way. Now, if these cherubim were, as we will find, types of Christ and His redeeming work, the meaning is very beautiful and clear. While the Fall has shut us out from Eden and the old sources of life, and we can no longer approach the tree of life through Eden, there is a new way to it provided through Christ. And we can approach it by way of the cherubim, that is, by way of the Lord Jesus, and through Him receive its life-giving strength in the measure of our need for this mortal state. Then by and by we may partake of His fullness in the resurrection glory of the eternal future.

Have we understood these things? "Therefore every teacher of the law who has been instructed about the kingdom of heaven is like the owner of a house who brings out of his storeroom new treasures as well as old" (Matthew 13:52). Have we received not only the truth, but "the Spirit who is from God, that we may understand what God has freely given us" (1 Corinthians 2:12)? We are in the Palace Beautiful; the Interpreter leads us, and as He shows us all its treasures, He stops and adds, "These things are all your own." Have we received them—the new creation, the Bridegroom's love, the rest of God, the flowers and fruits of His spiritual husbandry, and the life of Christ to be made manifest even in our mortal flesh? Then, indeed, for us is it true even now,

> "He who was seated on the throne said, 'I am making everything new!' . . . He said to me: 'It is done. . . . To him who is thirsty I will give to drink without cost from the spring of the water of life. He who overcomes will inherit all this, and I will be his God and he will be my son' " (Revelation 21:5-7).

CHAPTER 2

Emblems from the Story of the Fall

The inspired account of man's first disobedience and its bitter fruits is all too real and literal. Underneath the simple narrative there lies much deep spiritual symbolism and significance vividly illustrating not only the dark shadows of sin and misery, but also the whole contrasted light and glory of grace and redemption.

The Serpent or Temptation

We believe that there was a literal serpent employed as the instrument in temptation. Yet the whole language of the Bible unfolds with clear and emphatic fullness a mightier personality back of the ostensible agent to whom this name is applied in many subsequent allusions. The New Testament writers invariably speak of Satan under this figure, and the closing scenes of the Apocalypse unveil the vision of his final judgment and destruction.

1. *The Literal Serpent*

That Satan should come to our first parents in this guise should not surprise us and does not seem to have startled Eve herself. Not knowing yet all the properties and qualities of even the natural creation, she may have supposed that there was nothing extraordinary in the serpent addressing her. Never having been tempted before, she could not be expected to have been on her guard against temptation. For us the lesson is obvious and solemn that temptation will not assail us usually in its naked repulsiveness and in the undisguised form of its satanic force, but through some unexpected second cause. It always comes through that which we will be least liable to suspect. The traditional idea that the devil came to our Lord with cloven foot and demoniac form is contrary to the very idea of temptation. Such a creature would scarcely mislead or persuade.

An old Scotchman, looking at such a picture of the temptation, smiled sarcastically at the figure of the fiend, and drily answered, "Yon devil would never tempt me." Let us therefore be looking for the insidious approaches of evil, not in startling apparitions or extraordinary manifestations, but in the simplest concerns and most commonplace occurrences and objects of our everyday lives. We must ever remember that the price of safety is eternal vigilance.

2. *The Real Tempter*

We need not say that this was the devil; Isaiah calls him "Leviathan the gliding serpent, Leviathan the coiling serpent . . . the monster of the sea" (Isaiah 27:1). Paul calls him the serpent that deceived Eve through subtlety, and John calls him that old serpent, the dragon which is the devil and Satan.

The literal serpent is probably the most perfect type of his spiritual qualities. Of his history we understand enough to know that he was originally one of the most intelligent and brilliant of created beings—the "anointed . . . cherub, . . . blameless in [his] ways . . . till wickedness was found in [him]. . . . [His] heart became proud on account of [his] beauty, and [he] corrupted [his] wisdom because of [his] splendor. . . . [He was] on the holy mount of God; [he] walked among the fiery stones" (Ezekiel 28:14-15, 17, 14). He is the embodiment of knowledge without purity, of wisdom devoid of principle, and the most brilliant qualities of intellect coupled with motives most selfish, malignant and desperately wicked. Like the serpent, his chief resource is guile. His wiles are more to be dreaded than his direct assaults. It is evident from this record that his career of wickedness and ruin had already begun long ago. He dragged down with him in his desperate course the angels who kept not their first estate. Now he had come to wreck the purity and happiness of the fair new world that had just sprung from the

Creator's hand. Why God should allow, even for a season, such an influence to touch His creation, is one of the mysteries of the divine government, which is practically the same as the question in our lives day by day. This is probably a sufficient reason—that good must be tested before it can be rewarded, and that all character and righteousness must be devil-proof before it can be finally approved and recompensed.

3. *The Method of the Temptation*

His first word to Eve was an unqualified "Yea" (Genesis 3:1, KJV). It was a complete assent to all that he was about to question and deny—an absolute and utterly deceiving disguise intended to throw her off her guard by taking sides with her, in order that, from her own standpoint, he might bring her to his. Thus he ever approaches us. He always prefers to fight his battle from our side of the field. He would much rather work from a Christian pulpit than from the pagan press or even a theatrical stage. His very first utterance is an unblushing lie, and from that day when he said yes, he has always meant no. Our Savior called him a liar and the father of lies. The true way to understand and checkmate him is always to read him by contraries and treat his promises as curses and his terrific threats as the pledges of divine blessing.

His second word is a question. That has ever been his favorite weapon. He does not assail our faith directly, but skillfully insinuates the finest shades of inquiry. Then when he has lodged it, like the adhesive film of a spider's web, he proceeds, with exquisite skill and celerity, to weave around it the meshes of his fatal snare. His questions are always directed against the Word of God. "Hath God said?" (3:1, KJV) is still his favorite shaft, and it is never so effectual as when preceded and winged by the old "Yea" of the garden. The atheistic "God has not said" of Voltaire or Paine is not half so dangerous as the finely insinuating skepticism of Satan's chosen instrument in the religious pulpit and press. Our day is flooded with its arrows of false and fatal liberalism.

Soon comes the next stage: "You will not surely die" (3:4). The spirit of skepticism in regard to the inspiration of the Scripture is always followed by the loosening of the sanctions of divine government and the denial of retribution. Today there are widespread and pernicious teachings of such multitudes of so-called consecrated voices in denial of future punishment, and the attempt to establish a system of easy indulgence and boundless probation for the impenitent and obstinate. These are but the voices of Eden repeated in multiplied echoes in these last times, when the ages meet before the end and the prototypes of the past are receiving their last and highest fulfillment.

Let us observe that Satan's promise to Eve, "You will be like God, knowing good and evil" (3:5), was not altogether false. The devil does not always lie, else his falsehoods would not be credited. His statements have enough truth in them to float them; his drugs enough sweetness to make them palatable; his promises enough credibility in them to inveigle us into his snare. His victims do, indeed, become as gods, even as he himself had become, by renouncing the authority of God and becoming the master of his own will and the lord of his own life. But this is the very curse of our fallen estate, and one from which we can only be saved by the death of self and the resurrection life of the Lord Jesus Christ.

As we turn from this scene, what a sad and solemn picture is this first temptation. It was an Eden of delight, the rich inheritance of every blessing, the very hour of uttermost love on the part of heaven, and yet the hour of peril, the hour and power of darkness. It was the chosen hour of our tempter and destroyer; an hour which sufficed to wreck a world and overshadow a whole eternity. It is to our Eden that the serpent comes in the moment of our most apparent security. Let us "watch and pray so that [we] will not fall into temptation" (Matthew 26:41).

The Tree of Knowledge, or the First Sin

That this was a literal tree is implied in the narrative. The name applied to it may have been given because of some property in it to stimulate and impart a forbidden wisdom. But more probably it was so named because through eating it and thus entering into a condition of sin, man in his own experience obtained the secret of knowledge of evil and the difference between good and evil. It suggests the important lesson that Satan's chief assaults upon us are directed against our understanding and that we are in chief danger of falling through our intellect. The symbolic tree of evil is a tree of knowledge; the symbol of good is the tree of life. The devil's promise to us is superior wisdom; the Lord's gift to us is eternal life. The boasted wisdom of the world is foolishness with God; the chief obstacle to simple faith is the spirit of human reasoning and our overconfidence in our own thoughts and judgments. Therefore if any man will be taught of God, "he should become a 'fool' so that he may become wise" (1 Corinthians 3:18).

Rowland Hill used to say that the greatest need of many men was to amputate their bodies just above their shirt collars. Before we can be truly taught and led of the Spirit we must first be beheaded and then reheaded in Christ. Without Christ, the tree of knowledge is a curse. The process of divine knowledge is life first, "and that life was the light of men" (John 1:4). The knowledge of evil is especially to be dreaded. Innocence consists largely in ignorance of evil, and the sooner we come to realize it, the more surely will we renounce this forbidden fruit and reach the Scriptural ideal: wise concerning that which is good, simple concerning evil.

The process of sin and temptation in the mind of Eve in connection with the forbidden tree is as instructive as on the side of the tempter. First we see it as it touched her lower nature and excited her physical appetites. She saw that the tree was "good for food" (Genesis 3:6). This is "the lust of the flesh" (1 John 2:16, KJV) which John mentions as the first stage of sinful desire. Next she saw that it was "pleasing to the eye" (Genesis 3:6). This is the aesthetic stage, the contact of temptation with the psychical nature, representing the solicitations that approach our tastes, sensibilities, intellect and emotional nature. And finally it reached her more spiritual sensibilities—it appeared as a tree "desirable for gaining wisdom" (3:6). This represents the spiritual temptations with which the adversary still assails our higher nature, and with which John closes the trinity of evil desire, namely: "The cravings of sinful man, the lust of his eyes and the boasting of what he has and does" (1 John 2:16). All these three stages of temptation we see in the conflict in the wilderness, in the life of Christ Himself, in which He so gloriously conquered where Eve had fallen, and left for us the secret and pledge of victory.

The most solemn lesson that comes to us from this emblem of sin is the fact that in itself the act of Eve was one of comparatively trifling importance. There was nothing in the inherent quality of the sin that appeared to make it frightful. That eating of one simple fruit could bring very serious consequences naturally must have seemed improbable. Had it been an act of great profanity, bloody crime, or incendiary violence we would have been prepared for some disastrous consequences. But for a thing so trifling as the taste of a single apple to be the pivot of a world's destiny is indeed startling. But here lies the very essence of moral principle and the fine line which separates right and wrong as wide as the poles. Right is right, and wrong is wrong in no degree because of the circumstances or the consequences, but absolutely because of the principle.

The less important the circumstances are, the more is the principle really emphasized. When we do a thing or refrain from doing it because of adverse results that will follow, we are acting from some other motive. But when it is so unimportant in itself as to be disentangled from all other issues, and the act is performed simply because of the command itself, then it is manifestly a more perfect act of absolute obedience. The great tests of obedience, therefore, often lie in very little things. If we can disobey God in what seems a trifle, we exhibit the spirit of disobedience pure and simple. When we obey Him in the minutest trifle which we may not even understand, and whose consequences we cannot be capable of reasoning out, our obedience is most perfect and pleasing to Him.

Therefore we find that Saul lost his kingdom through one little act of disobedience, and the old prophet of Israel lost his life by simply going home to sleep in the house of his friend contrary to the divine command. On the other hand,

Abraham's covenant was established through an act of rigid obedience to a command that seemed incomprehensible. Eve wrecked the world by one little disobedience, and the issues of our lives likewise are ever turning on pivots as fine as the jewels around which the delicate wheels of our watches revolve. The root of sin in this sad picture is doubt, the tree is disobedience, and the fruit is death.

The Fig Leaves

The first effect of sin is shame, a sense of nakedness, a strange consciousness which makes even that which was innocent and pure, repulsive and wrong. When we disobey God, even the holiest things of life and nature are defiled. The guilty pair at once discovered that they had the knowledge of evil, and their sense of shame and nakedness implies far more than mere physical consciousness, for it was the beginning of an evil conscience and the gnawing of that self-reproach that constitutes the curse of sin. The instinct that sought a covering for their persons in the fig leaves of the garden is a symbol of the vain attempts of man's guilt in every age to find some covering for its shame and from its penalty. This may stand for the excuses and attempts at palliation with which the soul first seeks to avoid the issue and cover its guilt. This we see in the miserable pretexts and mutual recriminations of Adam and Eve in this chapter. Then the fig leaves may stand also for man's self-righteousness. This is represented in the next chapter by the offering of Cain, and in subsequent ages by the ceremonies and external services of earth's false religions, which can never cover the nakedness of the sinful heart or satisfy God's demands upon our perfect love and purity.

Perhaps more than anything else these coverings represent the innumerable devices of mankind to settle the question of sin and satisfy the guilty conscience through sacrifices, self-inflicted tortures and all the cruel and abominable rites of heathen idolatry. All these are but filthy rags from which the hand of inexorable justice will strip the trembling sinner and expose his naked guilt to the piercing eye and impartial judgment of God. Sinner, how have you covered your naked soul and satisfied your guilty conscience? There is but one robe that can hide your sin and cover your nakedness—the seamless garment of Christ's righteousness.

The Promised Seed

The first word of judgment in this dark hour was pronounced upon the serpent in the hearing of the two trembling sinful ones, and it was a word for them of strange and, perhaps, at the time, incomprehensible mercy. Her "offspring . . . will crush your head" (Genesis 3:15) was the first promise of redemption. The marvelous thing about it was the calm and infinite resources of divine grace which had already prepared this wonderful remedy. And, without one expression of impatience or perplexity, God proceeded to unfold the purposes of salvation which were to undo the wreck of this awful hour.

Had we been suddenly called to face such an issue, and found our kindest purposes thus blasted by the wickedness of our enemy and the faithlessness of our friends, we would have been overwhelmed with disappointment and indignation. But God is ready even for this issue. Ages before He had prepared His plan, "the Lamb that was slain from the creation of the world" (Revelation 13:8). And, reserving the judgment of the transgressors until He had first provided the remedy, He began to unroll the scroll of redeeming promise which, at the last, reached its fulfillment in the Cross of Calvary and the consummation of redemption. Marvelous riches of grace which loved us, even when we were dead in sins, "that in the coming ages he might show the incomparable riches of his grace, expressed in his kindness to us in Christ Jesus" (Ephesians 2:7). The language of this promise through all the veil of the symbol and figure glows with the very love and effulgence of the gospel. The very term *seed* suggests the figure which the Master applied to Himself as the great natural type of life through death. He is the true seed of all spiritual life planted like the kernel of wheat in the soil to die, but springing forth to bear much fruit in His spiritual offspring. The seed of the woman is the revealing of the mystery of the incarnation and the babe of the virgin. It contains a gentle hint for the comfort of poor Eve that her part in the Fall should yet be counteracted by her glorious ministry in the plan of redemption. The crushing of the serpent's head and the enmity which God proclaimed from that hour between the serpent and the seed was the breach of the unholy alliance which Satan had tried to form with the new race. It was the gracious pledge that the battle of human redemption henceforth was not between man and Satan, but between Christ and the adversary, and should end in the triumph of redemption and the defeat and destruction of the evil one. But one dark and sad coloring blends with all this glory and victory, and that is the picture of a suffering Savior. "You will strike his heel" (Genesis 3:15) is a vision of Gethsemane and Calvary and the bleeding and dying of Satan's Conqueror.

> He sank beneath our bitter woes,
>   To raise us to His throne;
> There's not a gift His love bestows,
>   But cost His heart a groan.

The Coat of Skins

"The Lord God made garments of skin for Adam and his wife and clothed them" (3:21). Back of this simple statement there lies a whole world of spiritual suggestiveness. Why should the skins of animals be taken for their covering when so many simpler robes might have been provided, without the cost even of animal life and suffering?

Why should death so soon follow, especially upon the unoffending creatures around them? The next chapter introduces the picture of sacrifice, and we see the bleeding, dying lamb atoning on the altar—the divinely appointed victim for Abel's sin. When was this rite inaugurated? Was it not at this moment when the plan of salvation had just been revealed and the suffering Redeemer promised? What could have been more proper than that our trembling parents should have been taught in the strange mystery of suffering and death on the part of the bleeding lamb which they were called to sacrifice, the meaning of the death they had incurred and the sacrificial death of Him who was to save them from its eternal bitterness? And then, as its blood was sprinkled on the altar and its flesh consumed in the symbolic fire, how perfectly it would have expressed the justifying righteousness of the coming Savior to take its skin and robe them with its covering instead of the fig leaves of their own self-righteousness!

A shepherd once illustrated this thought with singular beauty. One of his sheep had just lost her lamb, and he tried to induce her to take the care of another lamb, but in vain. Then he flayed the dead lamb and covered the living one with its skin. At once the mother's attitude changed; instead of rebuffing, she welcomed the little nursling, and with the most demonstrative affection gave it the place of her own. So in Christ's robe, united with His life and righteousness, we are ac-

cepted in the beloved and stand in the same relation to our heavenly Father as His own dear Son.
Dear friend, have you known the blessedness of
the man whose transgression is thus forgiven and
who has learned to sing:

Jesus, Thy blood and righteousness,
   Thy beauty is my glorious dress.

The Cherubim

The last and sublimest symbol of this scene was
the figure which God placed at the gate of Eden
under the name of Cherubim and the flaming
sword to keep or guard the way to the tree of life.
We are enabled to discover much of the spiritual
meaning of these strange figures from their places
in subsequent pictures and revelations. They
reappear in the tabernacle as the complement and
crown of the mercy-seat before the ark, and were
beaten out of the same piece of gold, implying
certainly that they must have the same significance. This imperatively points to the person
and work of Jesus Christ, of which the mercy-seat
and ark were the most perfect symbols. We find
them again in the visions of Ezekiel connected
with the gracious presence of God as He revealed
His purposes to save Israel and then subsequently
withdrew His presence from the sanctuary until
His plan of judgment had been fulfilled. And,
finally, we meet this symbol in the book of
Revelation as the four living creatures connected
with the throne and the Lamb, singing the song

of redemption unto Him that redeemed us out of every kindred, tribe and nation. There they seem not only to represent the person of Christ, but more especially His redeemed people.

Without dwelling in detail upon the argument for this opinion, it is sufficient for the purposes of this volume to assume that they stand as divine symbols. First, they symbolize the person and attributes of the Lord Jesus Christ as our Redeemer and Head; and second, as the representatives and types of His redeemed people. It is the glorious principle, so divinely true, that as He is, so are we also, and that the glory, which belongs to Him, He has given to us, and we will share. This symbol in the tabernacle and in the garden personifies Christ more especially, and in the Apocalypse of John represents rather Christ's people, thus passing in the great process of redemption into fulfillment in the glory and salvation of His followers, who at length share His preeminence and throne. Therefore, it is the type of redeemed humanity—first, in the person of its glorious Head, and, finally, in His ransomed and glorified people.

With this in view, the details of the symbol become most instructive and beautiful. They comprised and combined a figure with outstretched wings and four faces. The first face represented a man, and so stands for the perfect humanity of the Lord Jesus Christ and His people, thus symbolizing the human qualities of affection and intelligence. The second face was that of a lion, signifying the lordship and kingliness of Christ and His people. The third, the face of an ox, expressed the two ideas of strength and sacrifice, which were so gloriously exemplified in His might and suffering, and into which we must also enter in the fullness of His fellowship. The fourth was the face of an eagle, sublimely suggesting keenness of vision and loftiness of flight, and the exalted place of glory and blessing to which Christ and His followers rise in the consummation of the plan of grace. All this is so true that the early fathers used these four symbols as the signs of the four Gospels. Matthew represents the lion, Mark, the ox, Luke, the man, and John, the soaring eagle—God's fourfold picture of His Son. One by one we, too, are following in sublime procession and entering into the spirit of the new man and the Son of Man, the kingliness of His Sonship, the strength and patience of His crucified and risen life, and the intimacy and exaltation of His ascension and heavenly fellowship. By and by we will stand with Him in all the glory of His mediatorial throne and shine forth as the sun in the kingdom of our Father.

This was the ideal of redeemed humanity which God placed as a group of heavenly statuary, as a pledge of our future destiny, as the goal of our highest aspirations, at the very threshold of man's lost inheritance, and in the very hour of man's deepest fall and darkest gloom. So ever, when things seem the saddest and even our fears have almost overwhelmed us, the same unconquerable love meets our helplessness, lifts up our sinking weakness and points our languishing eye forward and upward to the prize set before us, purchased for us by the glorious Captain of our salvation. Let us rise to meet His marvelous love. Let us realize these infinite and external possibilities. Let us claim these divine resources and promises, and, from the gates of Paradise lost, begin the pathway which leads by the way of the cherubim to the closing pictures of Revelation and the open gates of Paradise restored.

CHAPTER 3

Emblems from
the Antediluvian Times

There are many symbols of Christ and the Christian walk in the antediluvian era, that time between the Fall and the flood.

Abel's Sacrifice

In the two sons of Adam and Eve human nature branched into its two great families, and these two races have since filled up the story of human life. The first born was, and still is, after the flesh. The type of faith and spiritual life came afterwards according to the inspired order, "the spiritual did not come first, but the natural, and after that the spiritual" (1 Corinthians 15:46).

Like the spiritual seed still, Abel was naturally weak. His very name signifies "a breath," and seems to express the thought of his frailty, as perhaps may have seemed fitting to his disappointed mother in his infant feebleness. His chosen occupation, a shepherd, indicates, perhaps, a quiet, thoughtful spirit, free from the world's coarse ambitions. And it brings him into the line of Abraham, David, and others of God's chosen ones, and makes him a fitting type of the Great Shepherd whom his own death afterwards prefigured.

Abel is the first definite example in the Holy Scriptures of the rite of sacrificial worship, and is mentioned in this connection in the epistle to the Hebrews as the first type of justifying faith. No doubt the institution of sacrifice had already been given to our first parents, but Abel is the first whom we see bringing his lamb to the gate of Eden, and presenting his bleeding offering on the divine altar beneath the brooding wings of the Cherubim. "By faith," we are told, "Abel offered God a better sacrifice than Cain did. By faith he was commended as a righteous man, when God spoke well of his offerings. And by faith he still speaks, even though he is dead" (Hebrews 11:4).

Abel's sacrifice, therefore, speaks to us through six thousand years as the keynote of the gospel of redemption. Other voices have spoken since, but his forever will be the first. His life was brief and simple, but this one act was enough to place its testimony in the very front of the cloud of witnesses and to give him throughout eternity the foremost place in the choir that will sing around the throne, "Worthy is the Lamb, who was slain, to receive power and wealth and wisdom and strength and honor and glory and praise!" (Revelation 5:12).

1. *A Type of Christ's Atoning Death*

Abel's sacrifice was a type of Christ's atoning death. He no doubt understood it as the ground of his personal acceptance as a sinner in the sight of God. The language used respecting it in the fourth chapter of Genesis seems to identify it both with the sin offering and the peace offering of the later Mosaic ordinances. The words of God to Cain in the seventh verse, which may be translated, "a sin offering lies at the door," would seem to give this significance to Abel's sacrifice. The reference to the fat in the fourth verse clearly identifies it with the peace offering of Leviticus, in which the fat was especially offered to God as representing his part in the offering of Christ.

These two offerings expressed with great beauty and vividness the effect of Christ's death in expiating and fully canceling our sins, bringing us into reconciliation and communion with God. The specific idea of the peace offering was that of a feast of fellowship between God and the sinner. He fed upon the fat of the sacrifice, and the sinner upon the flesh, while the blood made atonement and put away both the guilt and consciousness of sin. However fully these details may have been revealed to Abel, it is at least certain that he presented his lamb as an expression of simple faith in the atonement of Jesus Christ and was justified precisely as we are under the gospel.

2. *An Acknowledgment of Sin*

His doing this was his acknowledgment of sin. His act of kneeling at the footstool of mercy as a lost and guilty man, showed he recognized he deserved nothing but the judgment of God—the same suffering and death which he witnessed in the helpless victim before his eyes. This was what Cain refused to do, and the real reason why human nature ever since has also refused to accept the doctrine of Christ's cross and has found it an offense. It is the humiliating confession that we are lost and guilty. A man will not submit to this so long as he can vindicate or help to justify himself. Conviction of sin and deep penitence are involved in true faith in Christ, and form the first stage of the Holy Spirit's saving work in our hearts. And so, in every stage, profound humility keeps step with highest trust, and the cross of Jesus is God's chief instrument for convicting us of sin and crucifying us to ourselves as well as to the world.

No soul can see its Savior until it sees its sin, and then it will most deeply see and feel its sin when it beholds its Savior. We must take the place of the publican before we can take the place of the pardoned. The only ground of believing is when we are on our knees at the foot of the cross with the penitent's appeal, "God, have mercy on me, a sinner" (Luke 18:13).

3. An Act of Obedience

Abel's act was an act of obedience and submission to God's revealed plan of mercy as it had been already, no doubt, made known to our first parents since their fall. This was the gospel of that early day. In receiving it, Abel did exactly what we are commanded to do now, and what Cain and all his race have, through pride and unbelief, ever since refused to do. "Since they did not know the righteousness that comes from God and sought to establish their own, they did not submit to God's righteousness. Christ is the end of the law so that there may be righteousness for everyone who believes" (Romans 10:3-4).

Abel did not stop to reason about the matter, but he simply came in God's appointed way and was accepted. This is faith, and everything else is unbelief. Cain tried to invent a way of his own and perished. Naaman thought that the waters of Abana and Pharpar of Damascus were as good as the Jordan, and he, too, would have perished had he not afterwards obeyed God's very instructions. The Pharisees were of the same race, and through the pride of their unbelief they lost the salvation of their own Messiah. And so, today, the two classes are likewise following in opposite lines, the one taking their own way and the other submitting to God's way. Where are we standing? Let us yield our hearts implicitly to the obedience of faith. Let us submit ourselves to His judgment as condemned sinners and then to His grace as pardoned sinners. We can claim not only His mercy, but His justice and faithfulness to vindicate us as we meet Him on His own ground and approach Him through His own appointed way.

4. *The Merits of His Offering*

We are told by the apostle that Abel's sacrifice involved a still further element; namely, he believed that he was justified and righteous through the merits of his offering. Not only did he believe that he was a sinner, but he believed as strongly that he was a pardoned sinner. Not only did he take the place of condemnation at God's word, but he rose also to the place of acceptance and sonship, "By faith he was commended as a righteous man" (Hebrews 11:4).

Faith must not stop with the penitent's plea, but must rise to the song of the pardoned: "I will praise you, O LORD. Although you were angry with me, your anger has turned away and you have comforted me. Surely God is my salvation; I will trust and not be afraid" (Isaiah 12:1-2). There is no presumption in this; it is simply honoring God's own Word. And it pleases Him far better than our tears and pleadings after we have claimed the promise and the blood. His absolute word is, "If we confess our sins, he is faithful and just and will forgive us our sins and purify us from all unrighteousness" (1 John 1:9). Not to believe or take our stand upon this is to make Him a liar, and to add the sin of unbelief to the sins which we are confessing. There would have been no humility to the prodigal's skulking in the kitchen after his father's tears and embraces of reconciliation.

The good Francis DeSales was once visited by a poor, trembling sinner, who proceeded to tell him, with bitter tears, of his life of infamous wickedness. The good man listened, and then knelt with the penitent, and claimed the divine forgiveness in a few simple words of trust, and then, turning to the penitent, said: "Now, my dear brother, I want to you to pray for me and bless me."

The man was thunderstruck. "Bless you," he replied, with deep humility, "how can such a vile sinner as I presume to bless a holy man like you?"

"Why, my dear brother," replied the good saint, "you are a vile sinner no more. Have you not just been washed in the blood and clothed in the spotless raiment of the Lamb, even more recently than I, and just as perfectly as I? Therefore I want the first touch of your new blessing."

The man at once saw the position that God required him to take, and trembling for very gladness he dared to claim his place as a child of infinite and everlasting love.

Yes, this is indeed our place, "Which he has freely given us in the One he loves" (Ephesians 1:6). What a transformation! What a miracle of divine transition! One moment lost, the next saved. Once a child of wrath, then a child of God. In the same hour reeking with blood-guiltiness, and then whiter than the snow. Have you claimed your place? Will you accept this unspeakable gift?

> Helpless and foul as the trampled snow;
> To rescue the soul that is lost in its sin,
> And raise it to life and enjoyment again,
> Groaning, bleeding, dying for thee,
> The Crucified hung on the accursed tree;
> His accents of mercy fall soft on thine
>   ear—
> Is there mercy for me? Will He heed my
>   prayer?
> Oh God! in the stream that for sinners
>   did flow
> Wash me, and I shall be whiter than snow.

Abel received this consciousness simply by believing. There is no doubt, however, that God added, after he believed, a visible token of the acceptance of his sacrifice, which is expressed by the words, "The LORD looked with favor on Abel and his offering" (Genesis 4:4). So our faith in Christ's promise is also sealed by the witness of God and the stamp of the Holy Spirit upon our hearts, and also by the new place of love, honor and blessing to which God at once exalts us.

This is expressed by the word "respect." God treats us with divine respect. The moment we become united to Christ, we are the objects of His highest consideration. We are entitled to the regard He gives to His own dear Son. Our persons, our prayers and all our interests become infinitely important to Him, and every angel in heaven is proud to minister to our welfare and to wait His bidding for His sons and daughters. Oh! what a place of honor and dignity does Christ bring us to! "How great is the love the Father has lavished on us, that we should be called children of God!" (1 John 3:1).

5. *Suffering for His Faith*

But Abel also had to suffer for his faith. It cost him his life. He was not only the first witness to faith, but also the first martyr for Jesus. Therefore, the word "witness" and martyr are the same word in the Greek language, used in the eleventh chapter of Hebrews. Oftentimes our testimony for Christ must be through suffering, and sometimes through death. While we rejoice in the honors of our high calling, let us also be true to our testimony, so that not only while we live, but even "being dead" we will, like Abel, "still speak."

Cain's Fruits and Flowers

The firstborn of Eve was welcomed by her fond maternal heart with a name which expressed all the pride and promise of earthly hope. She called him "a possession." She cried, "I have brought forth a man" (Genesis 4:1). Alas, he was but a man—the true type of flesh and humanity. His life as a husbandman may perhaps have expressed, in some measure, his proud resolve to overcome the curse of the fall and to force from the ground by skill and culture something that would contradict or counteract the thorns and thistles of the curse. He was proud of his work, and no doubt forgot that the ground had been cursed for man's sin.

Not only did it become the sphere of his occupation, but also the symbol of his spirit. His heart and life were of the earth, earthy. He knew no higher religion than that which was born of earth and had no higher aim and instinct than its pleasures and pursuits. And so when the time came for public worship, the offering he brought was simply the fruit of his own farm and the products of his own works. He recognized no condition of sin or need of forgiveness, but treated God on equal terms, as one with whom he felt at liberty to exchange presents as with a human friend. He was not without religion, as few men are, but his religion had no recognition of sin, and therefore no need for atonement.

At the same time it may have been a very beautiful religion, as the religions without Christ often are. His altar at Eden's gate must have been much more attractive to the eye than Abel's. It was probably a tasteful rustic scene. Perhaps it was festooned with flowers and vines, laden with the yellow ears of harvest and the many-tinted fruits of orchard and garden. Maybe it was worthy of the highest ideals of psychical culture, which the same spirit today is employing in oratorical ornaments, musical performances, architectural decorations and all the splendors of a gorgeous ritual and imposing ceremonialism.

As Cain's offering had no recognition of sin, it also had no place for Christ. There was no symbol of the coming Savior, no figure of the atoning Lamb, no apprehension of the need of suffering and righteousness to satisfy the Holy God. Such is ever the characteristic of natural religion; such is ever the test of the true gospel.

To the old monk, in the vigils of his cell, it is said, the devil appeared in the most fascinating form. He looked like an angel and spoke like a god. He said, "I am your Savior. I have come to bring you the assurance of my love and the vision of my glory, and I want you to worship me." The saint was almost deceived, but suddenly he turned to his visitor and said, "If you are my Savior, I will worship you and adore you; but if you are, you will not refuse me the token I ask. If you are Jesus, you will have in your hands and feet and side the prints of the nails and the mark of the spear wound." In a moment the apparition changed. A cloud of blackness passed over his face, and with curses and hisses he vanished from the room. So we can ever test the true faith and the true gospel. It will ever have the marks of the crucified. Let us discard all forms of worship and religion which do not recognize fully our sinful and lost condition, and exalt with unmistakable definiteness the suffering and sin-atoning Savior.

Cain's offering was simply his works, the things that he had wrought with his sinful hands. It is the perfect type of every form of self-righteousness. They were unacceptable because they were the works of a sinful man and the fruits of the accursed ground. And so our best works are tainted by the fact that we who perform them are sinners, and that they spring from the soil of our human nature which is already under the curse. There may be varieties and degrees of depravity, but the highest degree is enough to taint our best righteousness and make it as "filthy rags." And so Cain was rejected, as every such soul must be in the presence of God. Where do you stand, dear friend? Do you still have your own righteousness, or do you have the righteousness of Jesus Christ?

This question is regarded by many as a mere strife of words and question of dogmas. But we find very sadly in the story of Cain that a man's faith is the real source and spring of his life and conduct, and that a defect here will be fatal in all the issues of character and destiny. Unbelief, in Cain, steadily developed into wickedness of the most violent and aggravated form and led to irretrievable ruin. The first step was simply self-righteousness and rejecting Christ; the second was malice, envy and murder.

Not all at once did sin grow into these awful proportions. The word of God to Cain, as He gently pleaded with the erring one and sought to hold him back from his terrible career, contained a tremendous figure of the progress of evil. "Sin lieth at the door" (Genesis 4:7, KJV), has been translated, "Sin crouches like a wild beast at the door." His sin was then but a young lion, only crouching for its fatal spring. As yet it might be conquered; "It desires to have you, but you must master it." That is, now you can subdue it if you will, but if you wait till it has made its spring, you will be destroyed. Alas, it became too late for Cain to resist, and the unbeliever became the bloody murderer and a heaven-exiled fugitive, branded with the judgment of God.

But there is one more stage in Cain's career. This chapter closes, not with a scene of eternal judgment, but with the bright and fascinating picture of the first human city and the scenes of early culture, wealth and sensual delight. Separated from God and lost to eternal hope, Cain, like others, turned to the world and became engrossed in its enjoyments and prospects. The religion that was born of earth, as shown in his city, terminates with earth.

The names of Cain's family and their pursuits are all connected with the various phases of wealth and culture. It was in his line that arts, manufactures, riches, and social and sensual pleasures had their birth. There we see the earliest types of physical beauty, musical taste, ambitious enterprise, city life, polygamy, and the panorama of earthly pleasure and human culture that have since grown into such vast proportions and have led men away from God and righteousness. It is the birth of mammon. It is the type of the world. It is the attempt of fallen human nature to find a paradise without God. It is the sad and mocking effort of the heart which has lost its inheritance to find a substitute beneath the skies;

and it will end, as the picture of Cain's city ends, in the same bloodshed and violence.

Enoch's Translation

Symbolic numbers and names have a very important place in the Holy Scriptures. We find both of these in the story of Enoch. He was the seventh from Adam, and seven is the number of perfection. In him the race reached its ideal type, and that which God will ultimately bring redeemed humanity to realize, both in character and destiny. And Enoch realized God's highest ideal in both. He walked with God, he pleased God, and God took him in a chariot of glory above the floods of death.

His name, also, which signifies "dedicated," was a type of his consecrated life and the root idea of true holiness; namely, single-hearted dedication to the will and glory of God. It is remarkable that the other race—the race of Cain—had an Enoch, too, and that Cain called his city after Enoch, his firstborn son. Does this not teach us that the world is dedicated to its aims and its gods with a singleness and strength of service which might well be a lesson to the children of God? Cain lived for earth with all his might, and Enoch lived for God with all his heart and soul, mind and strength. The life and character of Enoch were in bright and lovely contrast with his own age. Three thoughts give the key to the whole:

1. *Walked with God*

Enoch walked with God. It was not a self-constituted and independent holiness, but a personal contact with the Father, on whom he leaned for every step and supply, and with whom he kept step moment by moment, as we may still do on the heavenly pathway with our blessed Master. The life of holiness is not our life, but Christ in us, an ever-abiding all-sufficiency and presence.

2. *Walked by Faith*

Enoch walked by faith. Therefore it was not by works that Enoch pleased God, but by a life of trust and simple dependence.

3. *Pleased God*

Enoch pleased, and had the testimony that he pleased God. His aim was to please God. He expected to please God, and he had the consciousness that he pleased God. He believed that God accepted his simple-hearted purposes, and God witnessed to his consciousness the sense of an unbroken fellowship. So we may please Him, too. His will for us is not an inexorable or impossible task. It is a gentle and gracious plan adapted to our condition, fitted into the chain of circumstances every day, and made possible to us by the constant presence and unfailing resources of His Spirit and grace. Are we thus walking with God, thus walking by faith, thus pleasing Him, and basking in the light and gladness of His conscious and constant acceptance? Happy place! If it does not bring us to heaven in immediate translation, it at least brings heaven down to us.

The fitting climax of such a life was reached at last and was the most majestic interposition of God's power in the antediluvian age, as well as the sublime type and figure of the future that is awaiting the Church of God in these last days. Without the intervention of death, without fear or pain, and perhaps in sight of the generation to whom he had witnessed especially of the future judgment and the coming of Christ, the holy man was translated, like Elijah in later times, and like his glorious Master from the Mount of Olivet, to the heavenly world. Undoubtedly it is meant for us as a figure of the translation which awaits the faithful children of God at the second coming of the Lord Jesus Christ. While Noah's deliverance through the ark and the deluge is the figure of the destiny of such as shall pass through the days of tribulation that are coming upon earth and be brought safely to the millennial age beyond us, Enoch's translation represents rather the glory that awaits the watching ones who will be found walking with God at the beginning of this time of tribulation. "After that, we who are still alive and are left will be caught up with them in the clouds to meet the Lord in the air" (1 Thessalonians 4:17).

It would seem that this blessed hope is especially linked with a life of holiness and a fearless testimony to the second advent, both of which we see exemplified in holy and faithful Enoch. He lived a life of holiness, and he preached the Lord's coming; so God put upon his life and testimony this glorious seal. So let us watch and keep our garments for that day. When the marriage comes, they that are ready will go in, and they that love His appearing will receive the crown of righteousness.

Thus have we seen in these ancient ages the fullness of the gospel in type and symbol: the faith of Abel, the holiness of Enoch, and the hope of glory. And, in contrast, the unbelief which rejects the blood, finds its portion in the world and bears its fruits of sin and misery. The Lord save us from the way of Cain, and lead us and keep us in the faith of Abel, the walk of Enoch, and the hope of our Master's coming.

CHAPTER 4

Emblems from
the Story of the Flood

The deluge has left its impress on the traditions of all ancient nations and in the structure of the globe itself. The Greeks have the story of a flood as vivid as the Bible narrative. Assyrian inscriptions give accounts of an early inundation very similar to the account in Genesis. We read the story of the deluge also in the traces the waters have left upon the rocks of earth, so that the truth of this part of the Bible history is written ineffaceably in stone.

It is not historically, however, that we wish to look at it, as much as symbolically, to see what there is of the deeper truth lying beneath the narrative. It would be a great mistake to read the Bible only symbolically. But it is beautiful to see hidden truths below the history, and above and around it, like the nebulous light that surrounds certain stars with a cloud of glory.

The Flood Itself

1. A Sign

It was a sign to man that God is holy and just and pure and will deal with sin in righteousness. It was a great object lesson of His retribution for sin. It was also a foreshadowing of the judgment to come. It is a type of the deluge of flame that will one day sweep around the world again. Both our Lord and His apostles speak of the deluge as a foreshadowing of that coming day when "the elements will be destroyed by fire, and the earth and everything in it will be laid bare" (2 Peter 3:10). "As it was in the days of Noah, so it will be at the coming of the Son of Man" (Matthew 24:37).

2. A Type of Salvation

The deluge is not only a type of judgment, but of salvation also. The principle of salvation by destruction is taught all through the Bible. The deluge destroyed sin from the earth, but it saved the Church. It swept away the world of wickedness, but it was the very means of preserving the little flock. The plagues of Egypt illustrate the same principle. They ended in death to very many of the Egyptians, but they saved the children of Israel. The destruction of the Canaanites after the children of Israel entered the land of promise exemplifies the same truth. Their extermination was the salvation of the chosen people. The cross of Calvary brings us salvation from eternal destruction by the destruction of sin and Satan in the death of Christ. So in the Epistle of Peter we are told that eight persons were saved "through water" (1 Peter 3:20). The deluge therefore stands as a type of the great principle of deliverance by destruction: the salvation that comes through the love and power of God to His own people by the very thing that overthrew their enemies.

3. The Principle of Death and Resurrection

We learn also from the deluge the great principle of death and resurrection. Perhaps this thought could not have been embodied in a more definite and striking figure. In the flood the little church was buried in a seeming grave and came forth on Ararat as if raised from the dead. It was the great type of Christ's death and resurrection, and it points forward also to His second coming when the earth will have passed through its last baptism of suffering and come forth to the new age of blessedness and purity. And therefore Peter connects it with the deep spiritual significance of Christian baptism: "this water symbolizes baptism that now saves you also—not the removal of dirt from the body but the pledge of a good conscience toward God. It saves you by the resurrection of Jesus Christ" (3:21).

The Ark

This also has a spiritual and typical meaning. It

is the picture of the Lord Jesus Christ as a shelter from the storms of judgment and the tempests of life.

Jesus Christ, like Noah's ark, is God's provision for our safety from the floods of judgment. The ark was not constructed according to the scientific plans of human carpenters. It probably would not pass the building inspection of our day. But it was a welcome refuge when the storm came. It was built by Noah in exact conformity to the directions given to him, and it saved all those who trusted it. Jesus Christ has not been prepared according to man's ideas of things. "He had no beauty or majesty to attract us to him" (Isaiah 53:2). But He is a hiding place for those who trust Him in every time of need. In Him we are safe from all the floods of judgment that will come upon the ungodly, and from all the storms and trials of life. And He is the lifeboat alone through which we can reach the heights of heaven's harbor.

He is the One in whom we die, and in whom we rise again to newness of life. Noah seemed to die in the ark. It was only seeming, however, and he stood ere long under the rainbow arch in the light and glory of a new world. So we lie down in baptism in His arms. It is a symbolic tomb, but we do not die. It is in seeming only. He had the bitterness of death. We have the safety of it. We are as secure in our seeming death as Noah was in the ark. Through Him we enter into death, and we come forth in Him into life eternal. Was there ever a ship before that started from the lowlands of earth and landed on the mountain tops that touch the skies? None indeed, but the ship of grace that sails from earth to heaven. Was there ever such a voyage?

The Raven

As the fierce waves of the flood begin to subside, a strange figure may be seen above the waters, the only thing that is happy and at home in the wild conflict of the elements and the wastes of desolation. It is the raven that Noah sent forth from the ark, and it went to and fro upon the waste of waters until the flood had subsided from the earth. What a type of the great personality of evil—the prince of all evil, Satan himself. It is the same figure of evil omen, whether it is found in him or in his followers.

1. Restlessness

The raven is characterized by restlessness. It went to and fro, constantly, but it returned not again to the ark. It fluttered hither and thither with weary wing over the tossing wave, finding there its congenial element in the wild sea, the reeking carrion and the decaying vegetation of nature. It was a restless soul having no quiet and no repose. What an image of him who goes about constantly seeking whom he may devour. It is the image, too, of the restless, unquiet spirit of man. You can see this unrest in the spirit of the world, whether in the ballroom or in the office. In the ceaseless round of excitement he is ever vainly seeking for repose and satisfaction; but he will never find it until the raven is cast out of him and the dove is put within. In heaven he would have no rest, but would break every barrier in the wild struggle to get away to find his home in the eternal abyss of darkness and the society of other spirits as restless and dissatisfied as himself.

2. *Filthiness*

The raven is characterized also by great filthiness. It found a congenial banquet in that from which everything else recoiled. It fed upon corruption. The dead of the earth lay upon the waves, and they became its prey. There is a spirit akin to this also in man. It is a type of impurity in life or thought or feeling. The wild passions in the heart of man, the sensual desires that take delight in vile pictures, in unrestrained indulgence, in filthy stories, in abominable literature or unclean and idle gossip—these are the desires of the flesh. They are ravens.

3. *Melancholy*

The raven is a bird of great melancholy. His spirit is as morbid as the food he lives upon. He is the bird of despair. Edgar Allen Poe pictures him as sitting above the door of his heart and crying "nevermore." What a picture of evil restlessness, uncleanness and morbidness. May the dear Lord save us from this reality.

The Dove

There is another symbol in the ark very different from that. It is the dove. You will not find it in regions where the raven delights to dwell. It went forth from the ark with gentle wing and moved for a while over the wild waste of waters, but unable to stay in the place where the other found its home, it came back again into the ark. A second time it went forth, and this time it found an emblem of its own sweet spirit, an olive branch which it plucked from some springing shrub, and hastened back with it into the ark. A third time Noah sent it forth, but now the waters were abating from the earth, the flood had passed, and it did not come back any more.

All this is suggestive of the Holy Spirit and the heart in which He rests.

The three outgoings of the dove from the ark are all symbolic of the work of the Holy Spirit. The first time it went forth, it fluttered for a time over the waters, but finding no place of rest, it went back to the ark. So in the ages before Christ came the Holy Spirit went forth over the earth, looking for a place of rest. Failing to find one, He touched men here and there, but He did not always strive with men. He lingered with Abraham and Isaiah and Jeremiah and David, but He did not come to dwell in the earth because Jesus had not yet come. He was abroad upon the world, seeking a place where He could build a nest and remain, but He could not find it, and He returned again to the bosom of the Father.

A second time He came, and this time He did find something. He came during the ministry of Jesus on the earth. He rested on Him like a dove, and thus could linger awhile in the world. He plucked an olive leaf of peace from the cross of Calvary, and, with this token of pardon and reconciliation for the earth, He went back again to heaven, with the message that the floods of judgment were abating.

A third time He went forth, and this was on the day of Pentecost. The world was ready for Him now. The floods had gone, and there was a place in which He could build a nest, fold His wings, and rest. And now He came not as a fluttering guest, but as an abiding presence. He came to build a nest and rear His young.

Has the gentle dove got a nest in your heart? Is He rearing His brood in your house? If He has, the spirit of Christ is there, and "the fruit of the Spirit . . . love, joy, peace, patience, kindness, goodness, faithfulness, gentleness and self-control" (Galatians 5:22-23).

The Altar of Noah

When the flood subsided and Noah came out of the ark, he built an altar and offered sacrifices unto the Lord. This, no doubt, was by divine direction. God looked down upon the scene with satisfaction. He had long been disgusted with what He saw on the earth. He had smelled the stench of sin until He could stand it no longer.

He at last turned the floods of water upon the earth to wash it away. But the judgment was not sweet to Him either. It was all a great graveyard, and it was dreadful to heaven. But at length there was something on earth that pleased God. "The Lord smelled the pleasing aroma" (Genesis 8:21).

There are people today who call themselves Christians and are preaching in evangelical churches who either openly repudiate the doctrine of atonement by the shedding of blood, or so refine it that there is nothing but an apology left for it. They have taken all the blood out of the gospel. They have done away entirely with all thought of vicarious suffering for sin on the part of Christ. They say they cannot bear to hear that God would be willing to butcher His Son for the sake of sin. It makes Him like some wild Indian tiger. They cannot stand the smell of it—they call it a doctrine for the shambles.

How different is the story of it here in Genesis. When Noah's altar was erected and the bleeding victim was burning upon it, we are not told that God turned away in disgust—the odor to Him was as sweet as the breath from off the golden altar. He smelled a sweet savor. He saw that man was not better than he was before. He looked into man's heart and saw there the same black wickedness as ever. He looked at Noah and saw that in a little while he, too, would be drunk in his tent. Yet in spite of all, He promised that He would not again curse the ground any more for man's sake, "even though every inclination of his heart is evil from childhood" (8:21). He would not henceforth expect anything from man, for he was a poor, helpless creature. He would count on Jesus Christ. The cross of Calvary has been sending a sweet odor up to Him continually ever since. He would not curse man any more, but He would take him at his worst for Jesus' sake. From that time He has looked upon man's unworthiness as covered by Christ's righteousness and counted him worthy for Jesus' sake. When Jesus is brought to God as an offering, He looks at you in Him and smells a sweet savor. It is the sweet savor of Christ, not of you. Keep Him ever upon the heart's altar, beloved, burning with the fires of the Holy Spirit. So will you ever be sprinkled with the blood of the atonement and God will ever say of you: "This is my Son, whom I love; with him I am well pleased" (Matthew 3:17). Then, too, the Dove will hover over you and find a home for Himself in the surrendered heart, where Father, Son, and Holy Spirit will make their everlasting abode.

The Rainbow

The sublime and majestic climax of this series of types is the splendid arch spanning the sky as Noah looks back upon the departing clouds. What a sight it must have been to the eye that first beheld it. Nothing is more beautiful to the eye of a child than the lofty magnificence of the rainbow. It is the closing symbol connected with the flood. "I have set my rainbow in the clouds, and it will be the sign of the covenant between me and the earth" (Genesis 9:13). So the rainbow is a token that God's covenant is with us. We read of it in the book of Revelation as a complete circle: "A rainbow, resembling an emerald, encircled the throne" (Revelation 4:3).

There is a blessed meaning in this for our Christian life. It is the token of God's covenant with you and me for spiritual blessing. It is a type of the nearer intimacy into which He designs to bring us. It is a symbol of the covenant of His everlasting love, "To me this is like the days of Noah, when I swore that the waters of Noah would never again cover the earth. So now I have sworn not to be angry with you, never to rebuke you again" (Isaiah 54:9). Sorrow is the dark background on which He paints this token of His love. The rainbow is formed by a combination of light and darkness. The light shining on the small drops of rain is separated into these beautiful prismatic colors.

His grace can take the storm clouds and teardrops of our life and turn them into arches of triumph and jewels of glorious luster.

The time is coming when our rainbow will be a complete circle. We will not have half victories then as now. That which we have only half seen, and which has perplexed and bewildered us, will develop into a full circle of light and glory. We will know as we are known, and our sorrow will be turned into joy.

There has been a difference of opinion as to

whether the rainbow had ever been seen before. Possibly it never had. Science tells us this is nonsense. It says the causes which produced the rainbow must have existed ever since the creation. They may have and yet never have caused a rainbow. We do not see a rainbow every time it rains. God lets the light strike on the cloud frequently at such an angle that there is no rainbow. Could He not have kept back the sun and rain from ever getting in that position which would produce this beautiful appearance if He had so chosen? Undoubtedly He could. Perhaps for two thousand years all the causes of the rainbow never combined, but God held them in suspense until the right moment came, and then He suddenly painted it on the sky by flashing the light at the exact angle which should divide the rays into their prismatic colors and form the majestic arch for the first time.

Beloved, there are hidden causes in us which could, at any moment, produce spiritual rainbows. God has kept them back, but some day He will bring them all out. It is possible to be preparing every day a crown of glory for our head. We do this by patient endurance of trial, by victories gained through faith in His name. Soon God will let the light shine in on these troubles and temptations, and they will take on a different aspect, and be turned into triumphal arches and jeweled crowns on which we will gaze in raptures of praise and wonder. Thank God, dear friends, for the things you have not seen yet, the surprises

He is preparing for you out of the very heartbreaks that have been so terrible to you. When He wipes your tears away you will know that promise to be true: "Our light and momentary troubles are achieving for us an eternal glory that far outweighs them all" (2 Corinthians 4:17).

CHAPTER 5

Emblems from Abraham's Tent

When we look at the life of Abraham, we see many symbols pointing to Christ and aspects of the Christian life.

Abraham's Tent, or the Pilgrim Life

The first symbol we find in the patriarch's life is his moving tent. He left the wealth and earthly prospects of his native home and committed himself to the vicissitudes of a pilgrim life. Although an heir of the world, he was himself to have no certain dwelling place, but was to wander as a stranger on earth looking for a better country and "the city with foundations, whose architect and builder is God" (Hebrews 11:10).

The first lesson of Abraham's tent is that of Christian pilgrimage. Like him, the children of faith must also be separated from the world and live as strangers and pilgrims upon earth. We must confess that we have no continuing city here, but seek one to come. How little this is realized in the selfishness of modern Christianity and the worldliness of the professed followers of Christ is very sad to contemplate. It is not necessary in order to be in a spiritual state that we get out of the world or be isolated from its practical affairs. The real essence of worldliness is in the spirit rather than in the circumstances, in the love rather than in the possession of earthly things.

One may possess millions with a truly consecrated spirit and be a real miser over a few worthless treasures. The spirit of consecration requires that the heart be detached from worldly aims and motives and that we should hold the world as not possessing, and use it as not abusing it. "For this world in its present form is passing away" (1 Corinthians 7:31).

We should never have our hearts or our interests so invested in the things of life as not to be able, like Abraham, to emigrate at God's call to some altered circumstances, or even to fold our tent altogether and enter upon our eternal existence. Let us pause and ask ourselves, where is my life invested? Where is my heart directed? Am I living in a tent, or building for myself a palace of earthly ambition or indulgence which the hand of death will soon crumble into a narrow tomb?

But again, Abraham's tent not only tells us of the pilgrim's life, but also of the true hopes and eternal promises for which faith must wait, possessing now only as he possessed the land as a homeless wanderer. It was all his own, and yet will be his literal inheritance. But during his earthly life he found in it no permanent resting place. So faith must still accept its heritage and learn not only to hope, but also quietly wait for the salvation of God.

Abraham's Altar, or the Consecrated Life

Wherever the patriarch rested his tent, there he also erected an altar to his God. This was the expression in the first place, of his steadfast faith in the plan of mercy, which God had revealed at the gate of Eden, through the sacrifices of His own appointment. This altar represented to his piety all that for us is involved in the cross of Calvary and the blood of Jesus. This was ever the spring of his consecration and the support of his future hopes. He saw afar off the coming Redeemer, and trusted in His grace even in the dim light of the gospel as it was revealed to him in these simple emblems. More clearly afterwards this mystery of the Savior's death and resurrection was unfolded in the offering of his own son on the mount, and the substitution of the victim provided by Jehovah in his place.

For us also, the cross of Jesus and the simple faith which rests in His atoning blood must ever be the source and support of every grace. But Abraham's altar was not only expressive of the Savior's blood, but his own consecration. The burnt offering which he was accustomed to lay upon that altar was the especial expression of the entire devotion of his whole being to God, of which his obedient life was the constant pledge and evidence, and the sacrifice even of his dearest affections and divinest promises and hopes was the last and crowning proof. Abraham did not only leave his sins at the foot of that altar and lay himself upon it as a living sacrifice. Even the very son that God had given and the promises which were linked inseparably with him were also laid there in unreserved surrender and committal.

This is the last and sublimest height of Christian life, not only to give to God the things which we have called our own, but to give back and hold as His the things that He has given. It was this which God so prized in the spirit of His servant and for which He so blessed and honored him.

Such trust and such consecration need never fear that they can lose anything by this absolute surrender. Indeed, our blessings are never fully blessed until like Isaac they are given back as from the dead, and henceforth held not as our own, but as God's deposit in our keeping. Have we come to Abraham's altar? Have we left our sins beneath its flowing blood and accepted the atonement of its great sacrifice? Then have we laid ourselves upon it in identification with that divine sacrifice, a whole burnt offering unto God? Yes, have we even placed there our Isaacs of affection—even of divine promise and spiritual hope and expectation? And are we holding all, even our most sacred hopes and interests, as divine trusts committed to us for His service and glory? Only thus will we know the secret of Abraham's faith, as we enter into the fullness of his consecration.

In speaking of the intimacy with which He treats him, God gives this significant record, "for I know him" (Genesis 18:19, KJV). While Abraham fully trusted God, God also felt that He could fully trust Abraham. Dear friend, can God depend on you and your absolute singleness and fidelity to Him? Blessed be the glorious grace, we may take Him for this perfect heart.

Abraham's Seed, or the Faith Life

It was in regard to the promise of his seed that the patriarch's faith was chiefly exercised and tested. As first received and understood by him, the promise referred to his literal offspring. But as the covenant became more explicit and the light more clear, it extended into vaster meaning, and the promised seed became to him the symbol of his coming Savior. That this was so is plain from the apostle's language in Galatians 3:16: "The Scripture does not say, 'and to seeds,' meaning many people, but, 'and to your seed,' meaning one person, who is Christ." That Abraham so understood it is implied in the words of Christ to the Pharisees, "Your father Abraham rejoiced at the thought of seeing my day; he saw it and was glad" (John 8:56). So Abraham's faith and promises were all summed up and centered in the personal Christ.

So let our faith find its center and our promises always reach their true focus in Him who is the first and the last, and the All in all of Christian faith and hope. Let even our dearest earthly affections and expectations, like Abraham's beloved son, be linked with and lost in the person of Jesus Himself. Then, indeed, will all our life be heavenly, and all our heart strings bind us to His heart of love. But there is another most important thought suggested by Abraham's seed. His faith and hope were lifted beyond himself and the narrow limits of his own short life to find their fruition in the lives of others. They reached their fullness not so much in the blessing which he was to receive, as in the blessing he was to become.

The linking of all his promises with his seed was a constant challenge to the spirit of disinterestedness and teaches us that we, too, are to lose our lives in the lives of others, and find our blessing in being a blessing. Natural science teaches that the great design of every plant in nature is expressed in the seed and realized in the principle of reproduction. While we may value the fruit tree chiefly for its rich and luscious fruit, nature recognizes the little seed imbedded in the juicy pulp as the true value and essential fruit of the plant. And so God estimates us, not so much for what we are, as for what we may become in the issues of our lives. The tree is therefore known by its fruit, and the test and standard of the fruit laid down by Christ is, "thirty, sixty or even a hundred times what was sown" (Mark 4:20).

The promise was given to him in the form of two most striking symbols. The first of these was the sand upon the seashore which his offspring were to outnumber. This, no doubt, had special reference to his earthly posterity, the literal seed of Abraham that will doubtless completely realize in the coming ages of Israel's restoration even the expressive fullness of this promise. The second symbol was the stars of heaven, whose number and splendor modern science has expanded far beyond Abraham's highest conception. But even this will be more than fulfilled in the spiritual seed of the Father of the faithful. A great multitude that no man can number, as various in their spiritual character, and infinitely more glorious than the stars of heaven will yet gather at His feet, and prove to Him and the universe the faithfulness of God and the blessedness of trusting Him. The same splendid figure is used in describing the rewards and prospects of Christian service, "Those who lead many to righteousness [will shine] like the stars for ever and ever" (Daniel 12:3).

We also may therefore claim the same glorious promises and possibilities. This is the true aim and the most satisfying recompense of human life. When the applause or criticism of man is forgotten, when the transient discomforts or enjoyments of life are past, when the fire has tried every man's work, and the wood and stubble has drifted away in the ashes of the last conflagration, then it will be blessed indeed to gather out of the wreck of life the treasures of precious souls we have been permitted to save, and place them in His crown and our own. God grant that we may have such constellations in yonder firmament.

There needs not for such the love-written
story,
The name and the monument graven in
stone;
The things we have lived for, let these be
our glory,
And we be remembered by what we have
done.

Abraham's Seal, or the Resurrection Life

God's covenant with Abraham was ratified by a
special sign which is called the seal—that is, a
divine token intended to mark the importance
and certainty of the transaction and the stability
of the promises involved. This seal was the rite of
circumcision which from that time became the
distinctive mark of the Old Testament covenant,
the initiatory rite of Judaism. It was not a mere
arbitrary sign, but was fitted to express in its own
nature the most important truths. It was especially significant of that great principle which under-
lies the whole economy of grace; namely, the
death of the old and the resurrection of the new
life. Circumcision was the death of the flesh. It
was designed to express the great fact that our
carnal nature and our very life itself in its innermost center and springs must be crucified and
then divinely renewed and purified.

This is the same truth taught us in the New
Testament ordinance of Christian baptism, only
the latter gives more emphasis to the life as the
former does to the death side of the figure. This

might naturally be expected from the place of these ordinances in the two dispensations. Thus early and thus vividly did God begin to teach His people that the new life must be a creation and must spring out of the grave. And that man's fallen nature cannot be improved by culture or gradually raised to purity and heaven, but that the sentence pronounced at the deluge must be literally fulfilled: "I am going to put an end to all people" (Genesis 6:13).

Hence this figure of circumcision runs through the entire Old Testament as the picture of sanctification. "Circumcise your hearts," "uncircumcised in heart," etc. Have we learned this searching and humbling, yet blessed truth? And blessed it is that we may die to this sad and sinful self and live with Him who died for us and rose again. Have we entered into the power of His resurrection and been made conformable unto His death, and are we reckoning ourselves to be dead, indeed, unto sin, but alive unto God through Jesus Christ? Failure here has been the secret of almost all our failures. Thoroughness and faithfulness here will save us a thousand deaths in the Christian life and make our life a joy and power.

The day prescribed for the rite of circumcision was as expressive as the rite itself. The eighth day is the beginning of a new week, and thus expresses most fully the idea of the new creation and the resurrection life. God grant that we may know the full meaning of this ancient seal and

pass out of the seven days of nature's life into the
eighth day of resurrection power and blessing.

> If Christ would live and reign in me,
>   I must die, I must die.
> Like Him I crucified must be;
>   I must die, I must die.
> Lord, drive the nails, nor heed the groans,
>   My flesh may writhe and make its moans,
> But in this way, and this alone,
>   I must die, I must die.
> When I am dead, then, Lord, to Thee
>   I shall live, I shall live;
> My time, my strength, my all to Thee,
>   Will I give, will I give.
> Oh, may the Son now make me free!
>   Here, Lord, I give my all to Thee,
> For time and for eternity,
>   I will live, I will live.

Abraham's Name, or the Confession of Faith

The covenant must not only be sealed, but
claimed. Abraham's faith must not only be confirmed by God's seal, but also must "[certify] that
God is truthful" (John 3:33). When God commits
Himself to His promise, He expects us to do the
same as unreservedly. And so Abraham was soon
required to prove his trust by open and unequivocal confession.

The opportunity was afforded in a very striking

and significant manner. God required him to assume a new name, slightly modified in form from his old name, but signally different in meaning. The name Abram meant *the mighty father*, but God gave him the name Abraham, which signifies *the father of a multitude*. The first he could claim without involving any question of propriety, but the assuming of the other involved the confession of his future hopes and expectations. And when we remember that this was done at a time in his life when his age precluded the natural probability or even possibility of the thing he claimed, we begin to see how very real the test must have been. He was an old man, and his body was now dead. The hope of natural issue was contrary to common sense, and yet the adoption of the new name would necessarily be known to all his acquaintances and would require an explanation and proclamation of his unreasonable hopes. For one possessing his dignity and influence with his family and followers, this must have been naturally very trying, and the trial was rendered still harder when it was protracted through a long season of apparently fruitless waiting. But the faith of Abraham shrank not from the full ordeal. Not only did he profess his confidence in his Father's fulfillment of the promise, but he proceeded to act upon it as if it were already past. He thus became the witness of that highest of all degrees of faith—that principle which is, perhaps, essential to all true faith, of which the apostle says that it "calls things that are not as though they were" (Romans 4:17).

This, indeed, is the faith attributed to God Himself by the apostle in Romans; and on this principle He is constantly acting in treating future events as if already real. Thus His own dear Son was regarded as slain from the foundation of the world. Thus we are recognized even in our earthly life as seated with Christ in heavenly places and invested already with the dignities and glories of our future inheritance. This is the faith which God requires from His people and which He is willing to give them. And indeed nothing but the Spirit of Christ Himself within us can enable us thus to believe and testify. Again let us ask ourselves, what are we witnessing to in our lives? How far have we really risked our all upon God's promises? How much have we ventured upon His simple Word and counted the things that are not as living realities, not only in our hearts, but by the entire witness of our lives? Have we accepted His pardon and confessed it? Have we received His sanctifying grace and claimed our inheritance in Christ's fullness? Have we taken Him for our physical and temporal needs and ventured forth, without waiting for evidence, upon His simple and naked word?

It is the record of God's ancient saints that they were witnesses of faith. In the eleventh chapter of Hebrews they shine like stars—like constellations in the firmament—of the Old Testament. Will our names thus shine in the annals of this dispensation? We are writing the record every day. God help us to inscribe them as with the point of a diamond in the Rock forever and let the record ever be "I believe God," and "I know whom I have believed, and am convinced that he is able to guard what I have entrusted to him for that day" (2 Timothy 1:12).

Abraham's Vision, or the Trial of Faith

Sooner or later the test of suffering must follow every promise and confession. To Abraham it came in a significant symbol recorded in the fifteenth chapter of Genesis, the vision of a smoking furnace and a burning lamp that passed between the portions of his sacrifice, in the darkness of the evening and the deeper gloom that had gathered about his spirit. So for us the promises of God may be followed by the going down of earth's sun in deep trials and even the horror of great darkness which sometimes comes upon the inner sky, and then amid the darkness comes the fiery furnace of heart-searching anguish and suffering. The children of faith must be tested in the very fire. The more victorious the faith and the more glorious the witness, the hotter must ever be the flame, until it seems as though both life and faith must be consumed. But gold is indestructible, and faith survives and brightens with its trial.

There was another figure in the vision, and that was the burning lamp that shone amid the darkness and above the smoke of the furnace. This is the heavenly presence which never forsakes us in the darkest hour. It was the majestic symbol of that

yet grander figure which in later days came to Israel as they came forth from Egypt's iron furnace,
the pillar of cloud and fire—the type of the light
and protection that the Holy Spirit brings to the
tried and trusting heart as it passes through the
wilderness. It was in this hour of darkness and
vision of fire that God gave to Abraham the most
definite promise of his future inheritance, writing
in the vivid light of the furnace flames the very
names of the nations that he should dispossess
through his seed, and speaking of it all in the perfect tense as already accomplished.

Is it not even so with us? It is in the hour of
keen suffering that God has ever spoken to us His
greatest words, and burned into our vision with a
definiteness and vividness which faith can never
forget the promises that He is now fulfilling in
our grateful lives. Let us not fear the darkness
and the fire, but trust the more through that
which comes chiefly to try our trust. Suffering is
not always meant to burn out the dross, but often
to burn in the promise. Let us not think it strange
concerning the fiery trial that is to try us. It is
more precious, even to Him who sends it, than
gold which perishes, and will "result in praise,
glory and honor when Jesus Christ is revealed" (1
Peter 1:7).

Melchizedek, or the True Object of Our Faith

A mysterious human figure crossed the path of

Abraham for one brief hour and left an impression so vivid that it has remained as a prophetic vision of the coming Messiah, both in the Psalms and in the New Testament. This figure is regarded by many authorities as really superhuman, and indeed no less than the actual and personal Christ Himself living on the earth before His advent in human form, in order for a time to represent to Abraham what His earthly life afterwards represented to the world, His mediatorial character and work. We cannot accept this view without stronger evidence than the Scriptures offer. It would seem uncalled-for that Christ should twice appear on earth in actual personality. We believe that He did appear to Abraham in human form just prior to the destruction of Sodom and Gomorrah, but this was doubtless an assumed appearance. Melchizedek is represented as an actual human personage. He was the King of Salem, the ancient Jerusalem. He was also a true worshiper and official priest of the most high God. Probably like Job, he was one who had preserved the primitive faith handed down from Noah without corruption, and God used him as a special type of the official character and mediatorial work of the coming Messiah.

The apostle declares that he was without father, without mother, without descent. He must mean by this that his record is thus mysterious and unknown, that he stands across the course of time without introduction, a vivid and transient figure expressing in one brief glance the aspects which God would reveal to us concerning His Son. These are expressed by the name, position and office of Melchizedek.

His name in Hebrew signifies "King of Righteousness." His political position was that of King of Salem, which signified "peace." And his official character was that of a priest. He thus combined in his own person the two offices of priest and king, and the two qualities of righteousness and peace.

These are the four thoughts which constitute Christ's mediatorial office and work. He is our Priest and King, and He brings us His righteousness and peace. As our Priest He settles for us the question of sin and secures our spiritual standing and privileges with God. As our King He protects us, subdues us, governs us and guides us, and conquers our enemies and His. As our true Melchizedek He confines these two offices in one person, so that the King, whose majesty we might dread, is the Priest whose suffering and intercession have saved us from our sins and reconciled us to His favor. He brings to us His justifying and sanctifying righteousness and becomes to us the Lord, our righteousness. And He will bless His people with peace. His sprinkled blood pacifies the guilty conscience. His pardoning love brings us into peace with God. His gentle Spirit breathes upon our hearts His rest. His bosom offers us repose from every care and fear, and in the inner chamber of His presence we find the peace that passes all understanding. All this He represented to Abraham. All this Christ is to us.

Have we met and accepted Him like the ancient patriarch? Have we yielded to Him our worship and submission? Has He become our great High Priest, our supreme and glorious King? Has He covered us with His righteousness, and become to us our sanctification? And have we at the footstool of His throne received Him as the Prince of Peace, and found it true in our happy experience "of the increase of his government and peace there will be no end" (Isaiah 9:7)?

Such are some of the symbols of Abraham's life. As we leave them, will they leave us also on our pilgrimage for the better country which he has reached, and at the altar of sacrifice where he found all by giving all? Will they have brought us the vision of our seed, and sealed us with the secret of our true life, the death of self and the resurrection life of Christ? And will we go forth from them confessors, like him, of our covenant promises, even if it be in the fiery furnace and the midnight gloom of life's deepest trials? And, above all other lessons, greater than Abraham or Abraham's faith, have they brought us to the feet of the Prince of Peace and the King of Righteousness, as the Author and Finisher of our faith, and the Alpha and Omega of all our hopes and blessings?

CHAPTER 6

Emblems from the Life of Isaac

In the fourth chapter of Galatians, Paul gives us a key to some of the most important events in the life of Isaac, and along with these a principle which may be applied to other portions of the historical Scriptures as a key to their interpretation. He tells us that the birth both of Ishmael and Isaac was typical of the divine dispensations—the former representing the law and the flesh, the latter, the gospel and the spiritual seed—and that the expulsion of Ishmael and the sole inheritance of Isaac completed the type respecting the passing away of the law and the permanence of the gospel. He also applies the teaching of these symbols to the spiritual life of the individual Christian.

Authorized by this divine pattern, we will endeavor reverently to gather the spiritual lessons, not only of these facts, but others in the life of this remarkable character. More reserved and passive than the other patriarchs, Isaac is, perhaps, more obscure and less understood by most

Christians than any of the characters of the book of Genesis. But there is none that, when properly realized, impresses itself so vividly upon the heart and teaches such profound and searching lessons for all Christian lives. A life very largely made up of commonplace events, it is just the life that meets the needs, the failures and the testings of most of us. We trust we will find many points of contact with that which is most real and essential in our religious experience.

The Birth of Isaac

Paul declares that Isaac was born after the Spirit and according to promise. His birth was not natural and ordinary, but extraordinary and supernatural. Not until nature had failed and the hope of issue from the bodies of Abraham and Sarah was humanly improbable did God even promise the covenant seed. Even after this, an interval of testing had to come before the promise was fulfilled. His birth, therefore, was the direct result of omnipotent power, and so it stands as the type of that greater birth, which, in later ages, came through Mary at Bethlehem, even the Incarnation of the Eternal Son of God. This greater mystery and mightier miracle was distinctly foreshadowed in the babe of promise that came to Hebron's tent.

There is another miracle and mystery of grace which was also foreshadowed by the birth of Isaac—that is, the new birth of all the spiritual seed of Abraham. Just as truly as Isaac was born of the Spirit, and Jesus became incarnate through the overshadowing of the Holy Spirit, so "no one can enter the kingdom of God unless he is born of . . . the Spirit" (John 3:5). This is not a natural reformation, not the result of human energy or will, but the power of the almighty Spirit beyond the power of nature and after it has failed. "To all who received him . . . he gave the right to become children of God— children born not of natural descent, nor of human decision or a husband's will, but born of God" (1:12-13). Have we experienced this mighty new creation? Blessed be God, it is for us as well as Abraham.

It is not only by the Spirit, but also through the promise. It is not an arbitrary favoritism of heaven, but "all who received him," to them it is given. Would you have this new life which brings you into all the blessings and hopes of the covenant? Come to Christ and receive the immortal life which He waits to breathe into every living heart.

The Birth of Ishmael

Ishmael stands for the flesh and natural life and the bondage of the law under which it lies. When we speak of the flesh, we do not mean merely that which is gross, sensual and basest in human nature, but all that is born of Adam and part of the natural life. Ishmael and Esau had many lofty human qualities, and Ishmael's race today are more noble in many things than their fellows. And so the natural man is often a generous man, a cultivated man, even a moral man. The unregenerate woman may be a beautiful girl, a faithful wife, an affectionate mother, even a social benefactor, but this may be all mere instinct and humanity. This is not to be despised. This is not deprecated even in the Scripture. But it cannot enter the kingdom of heaven. The word "natural" in the epistles is literally "psychical," the man of soul rather than the spiritual man. This is the nature which all the sons of Adam inherit, and which sin has tainted and overshadowed with the curse.

Like Ishmael, the flesh is the firstborn and has already claimed its sovereign rights in every human heart, before grace appears upon the scene. It is into this home, where Ishmael has grown up with all his established rights, that Isaac comes. And so it is in the heart that has walked after the flesh that the grace of God implants the new life of regeneration.

Dear friend, where do we stand in this matter? Let us not deceive ourselves because our flesh is not the debased, gross and vicious nature which we see in some. Let us remember the solemn picture of the life which cannot enter heaven. "You followed the ways of this world and of the ruler of the kingdom of the air, . . . gratifying the cravings of our sinful nature and following its desires and thoughts. Like the rest, we were by nature objects of wrath" (Ephesians 2:2-3). May God fulfill the other picture to all who may read these lines: "He has made us alive who were dead in transgressions and sins."

The Expulsion of Ishmael

The position of the infant Isaac in Abraham's tent, by the side of Ishmael, was very similar to the position of the newborn but yet unsanctified soul in the conflict with its old carnal nature. We can readily imagine the innumerable petty tyrannies and persecutions to which the little rival of Hagar's child was constantly exposed. It is the type of the battle which goes on so long in many a Christian's soul. He strives in his own new strength, but often in vain, against the stronger impulses and tendencies of an evil heart. The picture is drawn in the seventh chapter of Romans with painful vividness, and ends at last in the bitter cry of the baffled soul, "What a wretched man I am! Who will rescue me from this body of death?" (7:24). The strife was ended in Abraham's tent by Sarah, who, realizing at once the impossibility of such a life, and the peril of her most precious hopes and promises, demanded the prompt expulsion of Isaac's rival. "Get rid of that slave woman and her son" (Genesis 21:10), was the hard demand, from which Abraham's sympathy recoiled, but which God's wisdom approved and confirmed, and which Abraham saw at last to be unavoidable. So Ishmael went forth to his own place, and Isaac remained the undisputed heir of the covenant promises and the peaceful master of the patriarchal nursery.

We need not say that this stands for the decisive moment when the regenerated soul rises

to its freedom. Definitely and wholly surrender-
ing the old heart to death and exclusion, it
receives the Holy Spirit and the personal Christ
to fight the battle henceforth in the victory of
faith, and possesses the entire Spirit in rest, purity
and complete consecration. It was not necessary
that Ishmael should cease to exist, nor can we
claim that sin is dead, but Ishmael was henceforth
outside the tent of Isaac, and so self and sin
should be likewise outside the citadel of the will,
and the sanctuary of the heart. Sin and Satan are
not dead, but we are henceforth dead unto sin
and alive unto God, through Jesus Christ our
Lord.

Let us stop and ask ourselves, which of these
pictures is the true representation of our inner
life? Is the feeble principle of divine grace struggling for its very life in the midst of all the con-
tending passions and impulses of our carnal heart,
persecuted by the flesh from day to day, like Isaac
at the hands of Ishmael? Or have we, notwithstanding all the pleadings of nature and sympathy, "crucified the sinful nature with its
passions and desires" (Galatians 5:24)? Have we
entered into the rest and victory of a single heart
and a sanctified spirit, in fellowship with Christ,
who henceforth fights our battles and garrisons
our soul?

There is a great difference how we capitalize a
single sentence in the epistle to the Galatians:
"The sinful nature desires what is contrary to the
[s]pirit, and the [s]pirit what is contrary to the

sinful nature" (5:17), is the sad picture of the ceaseless warfare between our spirit and our flesh. But "The sinful nature desires what is contrary to the Spirit, and the Spirit what is contrary to the sinful nature," describes the battle in which the Holy Spirit, not our spirit, wages the warfare, and always wins the victory. May the Lord lead every weary heart to the surrender and the decisive trust which will bring this glorious triumph. This is our right under the gospel just as much as it was Isaac's by the promise. Sarah, in this, represented the Holy Spirit, who is ever demanding for us our sanctified rights and pressing us forward to claim them. Let us yield to her pleadings, and "get rid of that slave woman and her son" (Genesis 21:10).

It is also implied that this deliverance brings us not only into the life of the Spirit, but into the liberty of the gospel. "If you are led by the Spirit, you are not under law" (Galatians 5:18). Until we reach this experience, the soul is ever acting in some sense under bondage and compulsion. Henceforth its service springs from life and love, and is "the glorious freedom of the children of God" (Romans 8:21).

Besides the application of this incident to the individual Christian, it has also a larger reference to the two dispensations of law and grace. Hagar and her son represent the Mosaic system, and Isaac and his seed the dispensation of free grace under the gospel. Like Isaac and Ishmael, the former has given place to the latter, and we live in the enjoyment of its light and love and holy liberty. Against the idea of returning back to the bondage of that law through the Judaizing spirit, Paul earnestly protested in his letter to the Galatians and emphatically taught that the spirit of the law would ever lead to the works of the flesh. It is as true today, and as necessary to be remembered. Mere morality and discipline must ever fail to produce the fruits of true holiness. They can only spring from the grace of God, the love of Christ, and the living power of the Holy Spirit.

The Sacrifice of Isaac

The expulsion of Ishmael did not end the trials of Abraham's covenant child. There was yet to come a deeper test and a profounder lesson, a test and lesson that have their parallel in every consecrated life. The command suddenly came one morning which consigned all this hope and happiness to the dark and inexorable decree of death. "Take your son, your only son Isaac, whom you love," is the mysterious mandate, "and . . . sacrifice him . . . as a burnt offering on one of the mountains I will tell you about" (Genesis 22:2).

We are accustomed to look at this scene chiefly from the side of Abraham. We think of the amazing faith and fortitude of the father's heart that could yield not only its affections, but its very faith and hope and all that was linked with God and the future, in blind obedience and submission, and yet unfaltering faith, to this strange and awful test. All this is true, and all is worthy of the high approval which God Himself has placed upon it. It was the supreme test of Abraham's faith and obedience. But have we looked at it from the standpoint of Isaac? Have we thought of all that it meant to that sensitive and shrinking boy? The strange and sudden separation from his mother's side; the parting that must have been so trying; the journey of three long days of suspense; that strange reserve of anguish in his father's face that could not speak, yet could not conceal the overhanging shadow; the innocent question, "Where is the lamb?" (22:7) and the sudden bursting upon his consciousness of the full meaning, as he himself was bound and laid upon that altar; the silent submission, all the more impressive because no word is given us of his suffering; the strange horror of seeing his own dear father stand above him with that gleaming knife; the awful moment of agony and suspense in which an eternity could be felt before the hand was stayed and the tragedy averted. It was the same to both Abraham and to Isaac—as though the sacrifice had been accomplished. The bitterness of death was past, and to all time and eternity Isaac never could forget the memories of that hour. He had really died in the surrender of his will, and his future life was overshadowed with the consciousness that he was as one raised from the dead. So the Scriptures speak of it, and so must they have felt it.

Not only was it the figure, as nothing else ever was, of the sacrifice of Jesus Christ by His

Father's hand for our salvation—a sacrifice which
had no arresting hand to stop, no voice to say,
"There is a lamb to take His place"—but it has an
equally important meaning for our spiritual life.
It is to us the symbol of the death of self and the
surrender of our innermost life to God which
comes oftentimes in Christian experience even
after that deeper life which we saw begun in our
last section. The expulsion of Ishmael meant
separation from sin and the flesh. The sacrifice of
Isaac meant the death of self and the dedication
of the will and life and being unto God.

By various ways the searching test is made, and
the soul is led to yield itself to His will. And, in
the hour of sacrifice, it will find its life, and
"should no longer live for [itself], but for him
who died for [it] and was raised again" (2 Corinthians 5:15). Henceforth it is easy to yield to
everything that God wills. The spirit has been
melted and bowed, the head has been laid low on
Jesus' breast, and the keynote of life is "not my
will, but yours be done" (Luke 22:42). And while
God gives back even Isaac, and gives His higher,
better will to each of us, it is henceforth quite different. It is so linked with Him, and so mingled
with our self-renunciation that it is no longer us,
"but Christ [who] lives in [us]" (Galatians 2:20).
Thus must we learn to lay everything, not only the
evil, but the good, on His altar. We must hold
even our highest hopes and sweetest promises and
divinest blessings and innermost life as His and all
for Him, writing upon them: "For from him and

through him and to him are all things. To him be the glory forever! Amen" (Romans 11:36).

The Marriage of Isaac

The wedding of Isaac and the wooing of Rebekah are samples of sacred romance as beautiful as the story of Eve, and are as full of literary charm as they are of sacred meaning.

The fact that Isaac had but one bride in an age of polygamy was a marked type of his illustrious Antitype, the Lord Jesus Christ, who is gathering to Himself His one spiritual and beloved partner in the fellowship of His glory and His kingdom. Isaac's bride was chosen by the most deliberate counsel and care from his own kindred in distant Mesopotamia. So God is calling out of this remote world a people for His Son, a race that is linked with Him by the kindred ties of His own blood. Eliezer, Abraham's servant, who was entrusted with the choice of the bride, is the striking type, both by his name and character, of the Holy Spirit, through whom God is calling and leading us to Christ. Like the faithful servant, the blessed Spirit comes on His long and distant journey to seek and find the soul that He is wooing. He meets us, as Eliezer met Rebekah, in our common life and in the simple incidents of our human experience, which often lead to the greatest decisions of life. As he laid before Rebekah and her family the claims of Isaac, and spoke not of himself, but of his master and his son, and all his wealth and glory, so the Holy

Spirit hides Himself behind His work and message, and ever seeks to reveal to us the glory and beauty and the claims of Jesus. As Eliezer exhibited to Rebekah, and even placed upon her person some of the treasures which Isaac had sent, so the Spirit not only shows us, but gives us the precious things of Christ and blesses us with the tokens of His love even before our full betrothal and unconditional consecration. Like that ancient messenger, He gently waits a little season for our answer, and then, like him, He presses the urgent call, "Will you go with this man?" (Genesis 24:58).

Like Rebekah we must each answer for ourselves. Christ will have no unwilling wedded ones, but demands our wholehearted and joyful surrender. "Listen, O daughter, consider and give ear," is His cry. "Forget your people and your father's house. The king is enthralled by your beauty" (Psalm 45:10-11). Rebekah's reply was as prompt and unequivocal as ours should ever be. "I will go" (Genesis 24:58), was the answer which linked her forever with the most glorious hopes and destinies of humanity. She had nothing to give but simply herself. That is all He asks from us. Her very wedding robes, and even the veil in which she was to be presented to Isaac, were brought by the servant and were presented to her before she met her husband. Clothed in Isaac's robes, riding upon his camel, led by his servant, and wholly consecrated to be all his own, she went forth to meet him.

What a procession! What a picture of our standing! Thus we, too, may wear the wedding garments if we are to meet Him at the marriage. He asks from us no costly portion, but gives us all He requires from us. While we are told in one verse that "the wedding of the Lamb has come, and his bride has made herself ready" (Revelation 19:7), we are also told in the next " 'Fine linen, bright and clean, was given her to wear.' (Fine linen stands for the righteous acts of the saints.)" (19:8). Her robes were "given" to her like Rebekah's and like ancient wedding garments at the very door of the king's palace. We meet Him in His own beauty and character and are accepted not for what we are, but for what He makes us and is made unto us. Sanctification, thus, is all of grace, for "we are God's workmanship, created in Christ Jesus to do good works, which God prepared in advance for us to do" (Ephesians 2:10).

Let us put on our heavenly raiment, and keep our garments with holy vigilance, "so that [we] may not go naked and be shamefully exposed" (Revelation 16:15). As when Rebekah beheld her lord approaching she wrapped herself in his veil, and so met him with a token that he could not mistake, so when we shall come to our Master, may we be found not having our own righteousness, but that which is of the faith of Christ, wearing the robes which all heaven will recognize as the token of the Bride of the Lamb.

The procession at length was nearing home, and Isaac had gone out to meet it. It was evening, and others did not see the meeting fully, as, clasped in each other's arms, they entered the bridal tent, and Rebekah became the wife of the chosen seed and the future mother of the Redeemer Himself. So, too, will it be in a little while; we will behold on the distant horizon the signs of home, but before we reach it our blessed Lord will have hastened to meet us on the way. It may be the evening of life. It will be the evening of the world's history. And our meeting with Him in the air may not be seen by earth's busy myriads, but we will know Him and He will recognize us by the tokens He has given, by the robe we wear, and by the witness of the Holy Spirit who will be with us still. Happy meeting! Blessed hope! True home! The eternal idea of every marriage feast and wedding veil and throb of earthly love. God grant we may be found in that happy company.

Isaac's Wells

The later scenes of Isaac's life are not quite free from clouds. In an hour of trial and famine he seems to have acted without divine counsel. He went down into the country of the Philistines, where he found abundance of food and had an extraordinary measure of worldly prosperity. But there he had no recorded instance of the divine presence, and he met with continual trouble from the inhabitants of the land. There seems to be no doubt that he acted wrongly in this. He has become an example to us of the needless troubles and unavoidable spiritual loss which will ever follow even tacit disobedience and the acting of our own wisdom, prudence and self-will. Isaac obeyed so far that he did not go down to Egypt. But he went a little out of the land. So we, without going into the world, may touch its spirit and get complicated with its entanglements in some things, and so have to learn Isaac's lesson.

The first trouble arose from the lack of water, and when they dug the necessary wells, or rather opened the ancient wells of Abraham, their enemies strove with them and claimed the prior right to them. The world will easily get the best of us when we fight it on forbidden ground. Isaac showed at least the power of grace in the spirit which he manifested, notwithstanding his mistake. He did not contend with them, but moved on from well to well, leaving them in possession, and calling the wells by the names suggested by his bitter experiences: "Contention," "Hatred," and finally "Room," when at length they let him alone. We will always find room enough when we, like him, pursue a course of gentleness and prefer a temporary sacrifice to an unseemly strife.

This quality of patience and endurance appeared more strongly in Isaac than any of the patriarchs and had its real root in the self-sacrifice through which he had passed on Mount Moriah. So they who have died with Christ once for all will not find it hard to die daily on the innumerable crosses of life's trials.

At length he moved entirely out of the land of

his sojourning and pitched his tent at Beersheba in the land of promise. Immediately, that very night, God appeared to Isaac in token of His approval, and renewed with him His covenant, while his servant came with the tidings that a fresh and invaluable well had just poured out its abundant waters in the camp. They gave it the name of the covenant that had just been renewed, and called it Beersheba, or "the well of the oath." So we will find that a decisive return to the exact line of God's covenant will ever bring to us deliverance from our troubles, the presence of God, and the fountains of blessing.

Not only so, but the Philistines were glad to come to Beersheba and beg an alliance with Isaac and his tribe. The man whom they persecuted and asked to leave their presence while he was on their level was sought for as a friend and counselor when he rose to his true place and separated himself from them. So we never can bless the world till we are separated from the world, and never can lift it up until we get on a higher level than its own. The men who are not afraid of losing their influence are the men whom God will give influence with others. The men who are willing to risk the loss of the world's friendship, for the sake of God, are the men to whom the world will go in its hour of need for comfort and help and heavenly blessing. Let us be true to God! Let us ever stand within the confines of our inheritance, and God will bless us and make us a blessing.

CHAPTER 7

Emblems from
Jacob's Pilgrimage

More than any of the ancient patriarchs, Jacob speaks to us. He comes nearer to our life in human infirmity, in human imperfection, in human worthlessness, in human suffering, trial and discipline, and in the grace of God, which was magnified by all these things.

God calls him a "worm," as a true figure of his groveling, crooked, naturally selfish and supplanting nature. But God gave to the worm the mightiest of names—the name of "Prince with God," showing that grace can take us in our lost estate and seat us with Christ in heavenly places, making us partakers even of the divine nature.

Jacob's Birth

The first symbol that comes up in the life of Jacob is his birth. We see here a figure of his future. It would seem as if in him there was, even in his mother's womb, some of that inborn spirit—

the beginning of that faith which afterwards developed so mightily. So Hosea says, "In the womb he grasped his brother's heel" (12:3), as if in some way he had that in him which pressed him afterward to claim the mightiest promises of God.

Jacob's Birthright

The birthright to the ancient patriarchs seems to have involved not only the headship of the tribe, but the spiritual privileges of the divine covenant. They seem to have understood in some measure—Jacob did, and Isaac at a later period— that there was more involved in the birthright than the mere headship of the house. Undoubtedly Jacob's mother had taught him the hopes involved in his birth and the promises which heralded it, and, looking down the ages to come, he may have seen afar the coming of the Savior and linked with it the hope of his eternal future. It was this that made the act of his claiming the birthright, notwithstanding all that was mean and selfish in the way he got it, an act worthy of the highest commendation. Had he claimed it by the rights that belonged to him according to the promises given before he was born, it would have been an act of the highest faith. It is the same act which we perform when we prize and claim the offer of our salvation and sonship in the family of God, and let everything go to secure it. This had been promised to him before his birth, as his mother had, no doubt, taught him, and he should have put in his claim and let God work it out. Jacob, however, mingled his own infirmity with the faith that would otherwise have been right.

He claimed the prize with the tenacity of faith, and then marred his faith by adding his own works. God counted the faith, dropped out the works, and burned out the sin with the discipline of suffering. And yet we cannot forget that he saw its value, and Esau despised it. Esau said, "I am about to die. . . . What good is the birthright to me?" (Genesis 25:32). Esau had no sense of the eternal future, or he would have prized the birthright above all earthly treasures even in the dying hour. Jacob saw the treasure and eagerly claimed it and made it his own. So you stand with Jacob when you claim your birthright. When you lay hold on your gospel rights. When you take with a firm faith, not only the covenant of mercy promised before you were born, but when you press on to take your whole inheritance in God— not only to be saved, but to be sanctified. Not only to believe, but to become an heir of God, a prince with Israel, and a partner of the glory of your Savior. This is the meaning of the birthright and the faith that claims it.

But while we imitate his faith, let us avoid his unbelief. He who believes enters into rest. He who works, works because he does not believe. When you are sure God has given you the blessing, you rest. But when you are afraid God will fail or Esau outwit, then you try to help and only succeed in hindering. Jacob's falls were caused by the crookedness of his own nature which God had to burn out of him. God help us to learn the lesson and so believe that "in quietness and trust is [our] strength" (Isaiah 30:15), and we will not only hope, but quietly wait for the salvation of God.

Jacob's Vision

We pass on to the third emblem of his life, the vision at Bethel.

It came in the darkest hour of his life, when midnight was around him, and a stone was his pillow—a symbol of the darker and sadder lot which seemed to await him. And yet it was in that dark hour in the wilderness, on that stony pillow, that the God of heaven was about to meet him in a covenant blessing. The vision of Bethel tells of God's first revealing of Himself to the soul that has chosen Him. Jacob chose God when he chose the birthright. But God had not met Jacob. Jacob was like us when we take the promise and have not yet seen the Promiser. You kneel at the altar and claim the blessing. You hold it by faith, but God always makes the faith a reality. The days pass by, and when He seems to have forgotten His promise, and faith begins to faint, then it is that all heaven gathers about you. You trust God. When it begins to grow dark and dangerous, when Esau threatens your life, when you are in the wilderness at midnight with the stony pillow, then God comes and meets you, and makes real to your soul that which was accepted by your simple faith before.

So it has been with you in the revelation of Christ's indwelling Spirit. So, perhaps, in the healing of your body. And so it has been in prayer for temporal things for which you have believed. Vision first, then victory. Faith first, then sight. Simple trust in His Word, and then God Himself in all the fullness of a blessed realization.

Jacob's vision was also a foreshadowing of the pathway of his own life. He saw a ladder, and the top of it reached to heaven, while God appeared at the top as the God of his fathers. How it teaches us that the only true ladder of life is one that reaches to the sky. Jacob's ladder went all the way up to heaven. The ladders of human ambition only reach a few years ahead. Man's highest ambition is satisfied when he can mount the pinnacle of fame or reach the fulfillment of some cherished dream: knowledge, friendship or perhaps wealth. That is the length of man's ladder, it reaches only a very little way. There are fifty, sixty, seventy, or as high as eighty years. But Jacob's ladder had scarcely begun then; it reached to heaven. Oh, you that are young and looking to the future and count so much on it, have you made sure of the highest issues of life and eternity? Let your ladder reach up to the sky.

And then Jacob's ladder was not only a long one, but it ascended step by step, rung by rung, not all at one bound, but little by little, moment by moment. So God is leading us on, step by step. Are you willing thus to walk patiently moment by moment, overcoming and ascending?

Again, Jacob's ladder rose out of the darkest hour of his life. And so our blessings are born out of our greatest trials. Is your pillow a hard one? Is your sky very black? Look out for the ladder. It is there against the sky. You will see it if you look up. Shut your eyes and ears to all the care, fall asleep on Christ's bosom in the trust of faith, and it will meet your vision with its heavenly vistas and its divine covenants of promise.

But the best is that Jacob's ladder ended with God, and it had God at the top of it, and God all the way down, holding it up that it might not slip, supporting the traveler at every step. Let your ladder be guided by His hand, not leaning against the cloudy tower of your ambition, but on the hands that were pierced for you. Have you never noticed a servant, or someone busy about your house, how they wanted you to hold the stepladder while they climbed it? There is One, dear friends, to hold your ladder while you mount to the heights that would make you tremble but for His everlasting arms.

And once more we are taught that not only is God at the top of the ladder, but the angels of His providence are moving up and down every rung, guarding your steps. So your way is under His direction. Every step is under His care. He says to you, as to Jacob, "I am with you and will watch over you wherever you go, and I will bring you back to this land. I will not leave you until I have done what I have promised you" (Genesis 28:15).

Again, Jacob's vision is the symbol not only of life's pathway, but of Jesus Christ Himself—the open Door and the only Way of communion and communication with heaven. Christ Himself has given us this interpretation of Jacob's vision. Speaking to Nathaniel under the fig tree (who seems to have been reading this very chapter), He says, "You shall see heaven open, and the angels of God ascending and descending on the Son of Man" (John 1:51). As much as to say, "I am the ladder of Jacob. It is through Me that heaven is open. It is on account of My work that the angels of God come, and henceforth it is not to be in the old visionary way, but through the flesh of the Son of God, that you are to have communion with God."

So God is not only at the top of the ladder, but all the way along. Jesus Christ comes from God and reaches down to man, a living ladder of human steps, saying at every step, "I am the Way. I am the Shepherd. I am the Guide. I am the Life. I am the Author and Finisher of your faith." Is Jesus your Ladder, dear friend? Your Way? Your Life? Is every step you take a step with Jesus? In Jesus? A keeping step with Jesus? A walking in Him as well as with Him, and a finding that He is something unto you, this week, and week by week, that He never was before? This is the blessed meaning. It is God at the beginning, God at the end, God all the way along, and God all and in all.

Again, we see not only the pathway and the ladder, but the covenant and the consecration. Jacob arose and on the altar consecrated himself—with poor, imperfect words, it is true—and if it looks like wavering faith, still God accepted it, and henceforth his life was linked in tender bonds with Jehovah's everlasting love. Have we made that consecration and claimed that covenant? Is there a voice saying to you, "I am with you and will watch over you wherever you go. I will not leave you until I have done what I have promised you" (Genesis 28:15)? Is it not safe to leave all in those mighty arms? Has He given you this mighty word, "I will not stop until I have done what I have promised you"? How terrible life's perils without it. How blessed with it. Have you said, like Jacob, "Of all that you give me I will give you a tenth" (28:22)? Or, rather, have you cried, "It is all Yours, and I am Yours, and You are mine"?

The Victory at Peniel

We see Jacob now many years farther on, but not many rounds up. He is about where he was at Bethel, and so God has to throw across his path a tremendous shock to arouse him to the true meaning of his life. He let a trial come that threatened the life of himself and his dearest ones. His infuriated brother with hundreds of armed followers was sweeping down upon him. Here were the little ones, and here the helpless wives and flocks, and the pilgrim with his staff was helpless against the mighty warrior. It was an hour of extremest trial. But poor Jacob was at it again, putting out his feelers, sending on his presents, and trying to coax the lion to see what his ingenuity could effect. Then there seemed to come over him a sense of his helplessness, and putting his dear ones in the hand of God, he went alone at Jabbok's ford.

It was night again—a dark night. There was not a star in the sky, and I am afraid he did not even see the ladder there now. But he had it out with God, and God came nearer than He had in Jacob's dream. Clouds and thick darkness are round about His throne, and in the darkest clouds you will find Him. But it was different from the vision at Bethel. The danger was nearer now, and God was nearer, too. Then it was God at the top of the ladder, now God was on the level of Jacob, wrestling with him, having Jacob in His very arms. Jacob was able to put his arms around his very God. God came very close to Jacob, because God wanted Jacob henceforth to live very near to Him.

That wrestling has much of mystery in it—that deep, convulsive struggle some of us can understand who have ever had a night of agony in which it seemed as though our very loins were wrestling, and the cords of our hearts were taking hold of something invisible. So Jacob went through the mystery of trial and came forth in the morning another man.

It is impossible to analyze all this without destroying the beauty. I took up a hyacinth blossom this morning. It was very beautiful and very fragrant. I took it in my fingers and pressed it, and the fragrance was gone. So you have to take the spirit of these things. There are lessons here that touch many points. It teaches us that out of the thing that is hardest, we often may get the greatest blessing. Out of the thing in your life by which you are nearly crushed, you are to have your grandest victory. Out of the thing that seems ready to conquer and destroy you, God wants to bring to you a faith that you never had before and a revelation of His love and power that you never dreamed of. That very thing you thought a stumbling stone, God means to make a pillow for your head and a ladder of ascension to His very presence. So do not wait until you get into a comfortable position, and then say that you will live a Christian life. "I am going to get a certain place. I am going to get things fixed up. Then I will serve God." Don't say that, but go to God and let Him fix up the things, and you will be a Christian through the very experience your trial and deliverance have brought you.

There is something else here that we must have to be strong in prayer. That is the element of intense earnestness. There is something else in prayer, I know—a rest and trust. But I do not think the rest comes before the throes of agony are past. There is something in prayer that takes hold of God and cries, "I will not let you go unless you bless me" (32:26). It is not weakness. It is earnestness. It is life. It is the throes and travailings of a birth that cannot come any other way. It is not doubting. It is power, and it will end in rest if you will let God have His way. This is the meaning of your distress and the burden that is on you. It is the Holy Spirit groaning within you "with groans that words cannot express" (Romans 8:26).

Do not try to work up a frenzy of prayer. That is offensive to God and good taste. But when you have the throes and the agony of Jacob's prayer, remember Christ had it, too.

And then, again, we learn at Peniel not only the efficacy of the prayer that overcomes, but also the element that breaks down. Jacob did not get his answer by struggling. When at last he yielded and fell prostrate at the feet of Him who wrestled with him, then he received the blessing. The angel touched his thigh, and the hollow of Jacob's thigh was out of joint. In his anguish Jacob gave a cry of despair, and he fell at the feet of the Mighty One, crying, perhaps, "Lord, help me! I cannot even pray any more." And God may have said, "It is done. You have your answer and your lesson. You have been too strong. You have tried to do too much. You thought you could wring the blessing from Esau, outwit Laban, and now propitiate Esau. You have tried to do things yourself, Oh Jacob! Fall a helpless child at My feet, and let Me be your strength, and carry you henceforth." As he fell, I am sure he did not go quite down. He fell into the arms of God. And as he went forth, though halting on his thigh, he was leaning on Omnipotence. He had not as strong a thigh, but he had an infinitely stronger Savior. And so, beloved, when we come to this place, too, where our strength is gone and when we have no arm but Christ's, I am sure that after that we can say, "I can do everything through him who gives me strength" (Philippians 4:13).

I need not say the answer came to Jacob the next morning. God came to him here, and Esau had to follow. The next morning Esau was there—but a tamed lion—with weeping eyes, and loving arms, and a brother's heart, meeting his brother with reconciliation and tenderness. God had done all that. We must have power with God first, and then we have it with others.

But the best of all was that Jacob was a new man. And God said as he rose, "Your name will no longer be Jacob, but Israel, because you have struggled with God and with men and have overcome" (Genesis 32:28).

So, brethren, we rise out of our trials, ourselves gone—the old man and woman canceled—wearing His new name. What you want to get rid of aren't the sins of Jacob, but Jacob himself. It is to leave yourself, and go out another person in the life of Christ.

Jacob's Return to Bethel

Jacob did not get his full blessing at once. He seems to have gotten away from it for a while, and God said a little later, "Go up to Bethel and settle there" (35:1). After our hours of prayer and victory, we may go back. You say, "I had such a blessing, but I lost it." You can go back to Bethel and dwell there. Perhaps you cannot go to the same altar, but you can be in the same arms. Go back to Bethel. Then God will finish the work, and the covenant will be confirmed forever. The failure of Jacob to do this fully was, perhaps, the secret of all his later trials. Jacob went back, but he did not stay there. If he had, I believe he would have escaped the bitter trials that followed. But a little later we read that Jacob wandered through the land again. And soon came the shame of Dinah's fall, the strife of his sons, the betrayal and sale of Joseph to the Midianites, and the wreck of Jacob's hopes for years.

Oh, consecrated children of God, it is a glorious thing to get over Jabbok, but it is a more terrible thing after that to go back! Jacob went back from Bethel, and for a time he had the bitterest cup that a mortal ever drank. I don't know anything sadder than the second failure after consecration. We read in Judges that after they had entered the Promised Land, they went back to sin, and their fall lasted four hundred years. Oh, you that have come, be sure to stay at Bethel. Raise your altar and dwell forever under the shadow of His presence!

The closing scenes of Jacob's life are full of instruction and comfort. At last it is all right, and standing before Pharaoh he can say, "All things have worked together for good." "The Angel who has delivered me from all harm—may he bless

these boys" (48:15). It was all right at last, and it
will be all right for us poor erring ones. But how
many sorrows we may escape and how many
snares we will miss if we will always literally and
wholly obey our covenant God and abide in Him!

Jacob's Grave

The last emblem that we will look at is Jacob's
grave. He was dying in Egypt. He called his family about him and his beloved Joseph, and said, "If
I have found favor in your eyes . . . do not bury
me in Egypt, but when I rest with my fathers . . .
bury me where they are buried" (47:29-30). So
they swore to him, and after a time the long
procession moved back again, and they laid him
in Machpelah's Cave. Jacob was looking to the
time when the trumpet should sound and the
dead arise, and he wanted to have his very bones
within the covenant of God.

Have you chosen your grave among God's
people—I don't mean so much your literal grave,
as the future, the resurrection glory? That was
the beautiful faith of Joseph when he died. He
commanded that his bones should be carried back
when Israel went through the Red Sea. God
wants us to look out for our bones—not as some
people do, looking forward to their funeral ex-
pense or a grave stone—but for the time when we
will rise again, and our dust will be glorified with
Christ and His ransomed ones, or covered with
everlasting shame and contempt.

Dear friend, what a life. How weak, how poor,

how wrong, how erring, how much it needed the grace of God! But the God of Jacob—how tender, how faithful, how good, how patient. And He is willing to be your God and mine. Let us take Him in the spirit of the old hymn, which has been the cradle song of our childhood.

> Oh! God of Bethel, by whose hand
>   Thy people still are fed,
> Who, through this weary pilgrimage
>   Hast all our fathers led.
> Oh! spread Thy covering wings around
>   'Till all our wanderings cease,
> And at our Father's loved abode
>   Our souls arrive in peace.

CHAPTER 8

Emblems from the Story of Joseph

The beautiful story of Joseph's life is the worthy climax of the first book of the Bible and may well stand as one of the stately and colossal pillars in the portal of the Temple of Divine Truth. It is one of the few blameless lives of the Bible, and stands side by side with Enoch and Daniel in its unblemished loveliness. It is full of the most affecting and practical lessons for our Christian life, and touches at every point our experience of suffering and trial as the children of God and the great principles of divine providence which God is ever working out in each of our lives. In the higher realm of typical teaching, it foreshadows the character and sufferings, the grace and glory of the Lord Jesus Christ with a vividness and power unsurpassed by any of the figures in all this wondrous gallery of divine symbolism.

We will glance at Joseph's life and character in

both these connections, with respect not only to our Christian life and character, but also to his great Antitype, the Lord Jesus Christ, blending both aspects as the changing panorama may require.

Joseph's Birth

He was his father's beloved son, and so he is the fitting type of the well-beloved Son of God. We shouldn't fear to claim the same place and fellowship in Him. Christ Himself has taught us that if we are united to Him, and He abides in us, the love wherewith the Father loved Him is in us also, and we are made accepted in Jesus Christ. It will make our trials easy if we always begin the story of our life like Joseph's, with this blessed certainty that we are God's beloved ones. There is something beautiful in the simplicity with which John calls himself "the disciple whom Jesus loved" (John 21:20), without the faintest consciousness of presumption. So let us press close to the divine heart, and love will usually get the place it claims.

Joseph's Dreams

The consciousness of his coming destiny was divinely impressed on the heart of the child, and with ingenuous frankness he gave the fullest expression to what must have seemed his extravagant pretensions and expectations. And although rebuked and ridiculed by his jealous brothers, he still persisted in his confidence and testimony. So upon the consciousness of Christ's early childhood came the foreshadowing of His lofty character and destiny even when but twelve years of age. It forces itself into His precocious questions and confession: "Didn't you know I had to be in my Father's house?" (Luke 2:49). Later, even in the face of His enemies, and in spite of their hatred and persecutions, He witnessed invariably to His own divine character and glory, until, at last, it cost Him His life. So also to the believer, God unveils, both by His Word and Spirit, the vision of His high calling. Sometimes the veil is lifted higher, and the soul is permitted to know enough of the divine plan to prepare it for service, to fortify it against trials and sufferings, and to inspire it for sacrifices and triumphs in the cause of Christ. So the great Apostle pressed on with the invincible cry:

I must visit Rome also. (Acts 19:21)

I know that when I come to you, I will come in the full measure of the blessing of Christ. (Romans 15:29)

I will in no way be ashamed. (Philippians 1:20)

The Lord will rescue me from every evil attack and will bring me safely to his heavenly kingdom. (2 Timothy 4:18)

I know whom I have believed, and am convinced that he is able to guard what I have
entrusted to him for that day. (1:12)

So also he says to Timothy: "I give you this instruction in keeping with the prophecies once
made about you, so that by following them you
may fight the good fight" (1 Timothy 1:18). It
was for the joy set before Him that our Master
endured the cross and despised the shame, and
we, too, shall overcome as we steadily hold in
view our high calling and our immortal crown.

Joseph's Sufferings

The sufferings of Joseph are preeminently typical of the sorrows laid upon his great Antitype,
our Lord Jesus Christ.

1. *The Sufferings*

a. He was hated and envied by his brothers because of his testimony concerning himself and his
claims to his father's especial love. So Christ was
hated by His brethren, persecuted, rejected, and
at last condemned and crucified, chiefly on account of His claim to be the Son of God and His
unfaltering witness to His Messiahship and glory.

b. Joseph was sold to his enemies for twenty
pieces of silver. And so the Lord Jesus was
betrayed and delivered into the hands of the
Gentiles by the council of His own nation, and
judged and condemned in spite of the attempts of
Pilate to release Him.

c. Joseph was separated for many long and lonely years from his fond father and was really given up for dead. And so Jesus left His Father's bosom, and even bore the very hiding of His Father's face and the anguish of His wrath and judgment on account of sin, and at last died under the dark cloud of divine judgment.

d. Joseph was exposed to the most powerful temptations from the world, the flesh and the devil, but resisted with inflexible fidelity to the will of God and the voice of His conscience. So Satan assailed the Son of God with all the allurements and solicitations of evil, but found nothing in Him. Of Joseph we have no recorded blemish or willful sin, but of Jesus we know that He was "holy, blameless" (Hebrews 7:26), undefiled and separate from sinners, and "[was] tempted in every way, just as we are—yet was without sin" (4:15).

e. Joseph was accounted guilty of the sin of others and suffered innocently because of another's wrongdoing. So Jesus "who had no sin [was made] to be sin for us" (2 Corinthians 5:21), and bore "the iniquity of us all" (Isaiah 53:6). He was crucified under the judgment of human and ecclesiastical law as a criminal, and was so accounted by His own contemporaries and judges. This is the keenest of all humiliations, to be assumed guilty of that which we utterly abhor. The shadow of sin upon the soul is darker even than its penalty.

f. Joseph humbled himself to a lot of the deepest degradation and the most menial

drudgery and toil, and did it willingly and with all
his heart, accepting his situation with beautiful
submission and patience. So Jesus became not
only "a man of sorrows" (53:3), but a man of toil,
laboring at His workbench, with sweat of brow
and weariness of frame like the poorest of men.
And, to the end of His life, He knew all the
hardships of poverty and want, weariness and
homelessness. "The Son of Man has no place to
lay his head" (Luke 9:58), was His uncomplaining
cry; "I am among you as one who serves" (22:27),
was His chosen place.

g. Joseph became the companion of criminals
in Pharaoh's prison. So our blessed Savior "was
numbered with the transgressors" (Isaiah 53:12),
crucified between two thieves and accounted a
malefactor.

b. Joseph was the victim of wicked men, and,
in all his suffering, he knew that they were held
responsible for their voluntary wickedness. Yet he
recognized in all his sad experience that it was the
will of God using and overruling the passions of
men to fulfill His higher ends of benevolence and
wisdom. In speaking afterwards of his suffering,
Joseph added no word of reflection or regret; he
saw the hand of God in every step and above
every sinful hand. He said, "It was to save lives
that God sent me ahead of you" (Genesis 45:5).

So the Lord Jesus Christ ever recognized His
sufferings and death as the plan of His Father's
wisdom and love and the chosen path of human
redemption, and yet at the same time involved a

no less degree of guilt on the part of those who wickedly ministered to His destruction. Peter declares in the beginning of Acts: "This man was handed over to you by God's set purpose and foreknowledge; and you, with the help of wicked men, put him to death by nailing him to the cross" (2:23). And so the Lord Himself declared to His earthly judge, "You would have no power over me if it were not given to you from above" (John 19:11). Yet with strange solemnity He added, in the very spirit of the truth we have just stated, "Therefore, the one who handed me over to you is guilty of a greater sin" (19:11).

i. The sufferings of Joseph were not lost, but were the means in God's marvelous providence of saving his house and the whole world from death. And so the type is transcendently fulfilled in the glory and eternal issues of Christ's cross and shame, in the salvation of myriads of the redeemed from eternal death. It was this that enabled Him on the threshold of that cross to cry, "Unless a kernel of wheat falls to the ground and dies, it remains only a single seed. But if it dies, it produces many seeds" (12:24). "The hour has come for the Son of Man to be glorified" (12:23). "But I, when I am lifted up from the earth, will draw all men to myself" (12:32).

2. *The Application*

Turning now to the application of all this to our own lives, we find in Joseph's sufferings a beautiful example of the spirit a Christian should exemplify under trial and affliction.

a. Like Joseph, our sufferings may often come from our own brethren. Many of the bitterest cups of our lives are put to our lips by the hands of those we love. When men attempt to polish a diamond, they use either another diamond or diamond dust, and so God has to purify us by the hard attrition of our dearest friends and often our fellow Christians. Will we not, like Joseph, see His hand above theirs, and take our lesson and hold our victory?

b. Like Joseph, we must also expect to be tried, misunderstood, hated, persecuted and wronged by the world. We should not expect less than our Master, "If they persecuted me, they will persecute you also" (15:20). The secret of victory lies in the spirit of integrity and an unfailing confidence in God as One who is mightier than the world. That will "make your righteousness shine like the dawn, the justice of your cause like the noonday sun" (Psalm 37:6). "So then, those who suffer according to God's will should commit themselves to their faithful Creator and continue to do good" (1 Peter 4:19).

c. Like Joseph's, our sufferings will often come to us through the grossest injustice on the part of men, involving loss, and even shameful reproach. The verdicts of public opinion and human authority are not always equitable, and many of God's dearest children have lived long under the ban of the severest injustice. This seems at first to human nature very hard to bear, and yet the apostle has said it is better to suffer for well doing than for ill doing.

> But if you suffer for doing good and you endure it, this is commendable before God. To this you were called, because Christ suffered for you, leaving you an example, that you should follow in his steps. . . . When they hurled their insults at him, he did not retaliate; when he suffered, he made no threats. Instead, he entrusted himself to him who judges justly. (2:20-21, 23)

d. Like Joseph's, our sufferings may be aggravated and prolonged by the neglect and ingratitude of others, and even those whom we have most kindly befriended. The fellow prisoner, whose release Joseph predicted, forgot him the moment he returned to his place and escaped his own misery and left Joseph languishing in his neglected prison for years, when one word would have set him free. So our hearts will often ache at the inhumanity of men and the ingratitude of friends. Oftentimes we will find our best services unappreciated and unrequited, and will even be cruelly stung by those we have benefitted or even saved. How much suffering there is even among God's children which one word would avert or the smallest sacrifice would prevent! But we must learn to endure and to wait, to render every ministry unto God, rather than to men, and accept our recompense not from human gratitude, but from our Master's righteous hand.

How exquisite the answer of the great Christian soldier, who, when parched with thirst after a bloody battle, was handed a cup of water by his attendant. As he was about to hold it to his famished lips, he saw the hungry eyes of a wounded enemy looking at the water. Hastening to his side, he handed him the cup, but the man, instead of taking it, by a quick movement tried to strike his noble benefactor with a death wound in return for his love. The brave officer sprang back and saved his life. His attendant, with fierce indignation, raised his sword and was about to bury it in the body of the miscreant. But the good man held him back, took his sword from his hand and disarmed the wounded enemy. Then handing the cup of water to his attendant, quietly added: "Give it to him all the same." So let us love and bless.

e. The hardest ingredient in suffering is often time. A short, sharp pain is easily borne. But when a sorrow drags its weary weight through long monotonous years, and day after day returns with the same dull routine of hopeless agony, the heart loses its spring, and without the grace of God is sure to sink into the very sullenness of despair. Joseph's was a long trial, and God often has to burn His lessons into the depths of our being by the fires of protracted pain. "He will sit as a refiner and purifier of silver" (Malachi 3:3), but He knows how long, and like a true goldsmith, He stops the

fires the moment He sees His image in the glowing metal. "Perseverance must finish its work so
that you may be mature and complete, not lacking
anything!" (James 1:4). "The God of all grace, who
called you to his eternal glory in Christ, after you
have suffered a little while, will himself restore you
and make you strong, firm and steadfast. To him
be the power for ever and ever. Amen" (1 Peter
5:10).

f. Like Joseph, let us meet our sufferings in a
spirit of courageous cheerfulness and make the
best of them. Joseph might have given up and
said, "There is no use trying; everything is against
me," as many a young man is tempted to do in
adversity. But Joseph went into Potiphar's
kitchen, not to repine and fret, but to be bright
and useful and do his very best. And he so succeeded that before long he had the highest place
in the household. Then, when the scene was
changed from the kitchen to the prison, Joseph
again, instead of giving up in sullen despair, and
feeling that there was no use trying, resolved to
make the best of this position. He so succeeded
there that before long he was chief of the
prisoners. Wherever he found himself he did his
best, and having succeeded in a pantry and a
prison, he was ready for a palace and a throne.
The man who cannot succeed in a trying position
is not fit for an easier one. This lesson of Joseph's
life takes hold, as no other in the Scriptures, of
the practical questions that meet every man, and
especially every young man, in the battle of life.

g. Like Joseph, we will find it indispensable in the time of trouble to retain our integrity as a jewel above all price. We should keep our conscience so pure that by well doing we will be able to silence the ignorance of foolish men and give the devil no place for his assaults upon our faith. Joseph's heart would surely have been crushed, if, in the dark hour he had been compelled to say like his brothers afterwards, "I have been guilty, therefore this distress has come upon me" (see Genesis 42:21). If we have been guilty in anything, let it be quickly rectified, and it will be forgiven. Then, with a pure conscience and a true heart, we can stand against all the storms of trials.

h. The support of Joseph in his trial was the confidence and consciousness of the divine presence and the constant assurance which sprang from his early faith that God's hand was overruling all his life. There can be no doubt that in these dark hours his early dreams ever shone like a pole star of hope upon the midnight sky, and, as Christ, "for the joy set before him endured the cross, scorning its shame" (Hebrews 12:2). We must hold fast to our faith and hope, or we cannot overcome the billows of sorrow. We must ever recognize the hand of infinite love in all our trials, and never for an instant listen to the devil's whisper, "The Lord has brought us here that He might destroy us." But faith's answer ever is: "God is our refuge and strength, an ever-present help in trouble. Therefore we will not fear, though the earth give way and the mountains fall into the heart of the sea" (Psalm 46:1-2). "Because the Sovereign LORD helps me . . . I have set my face like flint, and I know I will not be put to shame" (Isaiah 50:7).

We may not see now the outcome of the beautiful plan which God is hiding in the shadow of His hand. It yet may be long concealed. But faith may be sure that He is sitting on the throne calmly awaiting the hour when with adoring rapture we will say, "All things have worked together for good."

i. Like Joseph, let us be more careful to learn all the lessons in the school of sorrow, than we are anxious for the hour of deliverance. There is a "need be" for every lesson, and when we are ready, our deliverance will surely come, and we will find that we could not have stood in our place of higher service without the very things that were taught us in the ordeal. God is educating us for the future for higher service and nobler blessings. If we have the qualities that fit us for a throne, all earth and hell cannot keep us from it when God's time has come. We cannot see it now, but surely will find in God's "afterwards" the benefits and the necessity of the discipline which His patient love has held us to so strictly, and yet so wisely, in the experience of life.

Joseph's Exaltation

The startling suddenness and transcendent greatness of the change which passed over Joseph's life in a few hours, seems almost too romantic to be true, but such transitions are not so sudden as they seem. Joseph had been quietly prepared for all this through the preceding years, and had learned his lessons so well that the mere outward circumstances of his promotion were much less to him than they seemed to others. He recognized in his new position a divine call to a new service, a situation requiring new duties and divine support, and proceeded to fulfill his new responsibilities with the same simple fidelity he had shown in his humbler positions.

While virtually the ruler of Egypt and the entire world, he used his high trust as a place of service and went throughout the whole land of Egypt with the same painstaking care as one of his humblest subordinates. The change that came to Joseph was sudden and complete. His prison was exchanged for a palace, his shame for the highest honor, his position of degradation for one of authority and prominence, and his lonely, suffering life for a happy home and the fellowship of a beloved and noble wife and family. As the years rolled on, all that was lost was restored. The broken ties of home were healed; his dear father and fond brother were given back to his arms. The very brothers that had betrayed him were reconciled to his affections. They were made to see the sin and folly of their crime in a manner so wonderful and delightful that it took out of the past every bitter memory and painful sting, and the saddest trials he had known were turned into the sweetest blessings of his life and others. The which to him was the highest of all enjoyments, the opportunity of returning good for evil, ministering to the happiness of those he loved, cherishing and nourishing his father's house and his brethren with all the riches of his glory, and seeing them and the entire world blessed and even saved through the ministry of his suffering life. Surely this was, indeed, a transformation of suffering into glory and blessing.

1. *His Exaltation—a Type of Christ*

All this was the type of Christ's exaltation and the pledge of our reward.

a. It foreshadows the exaltation of Jesus, after the shame and suffering of the cross, to the resurrection life and heavenly glory upon which He entered.

b. The relation of Joseph to Pharaoh suggests the mediatorial office of Jesus Christ with the Father, administering as He does the government of the universe, and having all things delivered into His hands. Pharaoh answered every petition that came to him with the message, "Go to Joseph!" and so we have access unto the Father through Him, and receive the riches of grace and the blessings which we need and claim. All the treasures of Egypt were in Joseph's hands. All the store, which saved and fed the famishing people, was given out at his orders. Likewise Scripture says of Christ, "God was pleased to have all his fullness dwell in him" (Colossians 1:19); "and from the fullness of his grace we have all received one blessing after another" (John 1:16).

c. Joseph was virtually ruler over the land of Egypt and the entire world, and so Christ has been invested with like power in heaven and in earth. He is established "far above all . . . power and dominion, and every title that can be given, not only in the present age but also in the one to come. And God placed all things under his feet and appointed him to be head over everything for the church" (Ephesians 1:21-22). Let us ever remember, when we look at the forces around us and our bitter trials, that

> He everywhere hath sway,
>   And all things serve His might;
> His every act pure blessing is,
>   His path unsullied light.

d. The marriage of Joseph, after his exaltation, has been applied by some interpreters to the gathering of Christ's Church to Himself in the heavenly places. It was not during His life of shame and suffering, but after His ascension, that He established the Church and her true place with Him—even in the present dispensation. The place where she should ever recognize herself as sitting is by His side in glory. This also is part of His glory and is to be His eternal joy, the Church of His love and the partner of His nature and His throne.

e. The years of plenty, and then the years of famine which followed them, seem to foreshadow two things. First, the dispensation of grace which is now proceeding; and second, the time of tribulation which is coming upon the earth before the end, out of which He will gather His people to meet Him in the air. It was during this time of famine that Joseph's brothers came to him and were reconciled. And so will it be during the days of tribulation that Christ's brethren after the flesh, the Jews, will recognize Him. They will repent of their sins, and be restored to His friendship and blessing, and afterwards share with Him in their own separate national life, as in Egypt of old, the blessing of His millennial kingdom. This is to be one of the crowning glories of the once rejected Nazarene: "They will look on me, the one they have pierced, and they will mourn" (Zechariah 12:10). They will be reconciled to the Messiah that they delivered to the Gentiles, and who God has made such a blessing to the Gentiles, as He made Joseph of old. This whole story, therefore, is the picture in some degree at least, of the millennial times, and no doubt the fulfillment will bring out many resemblances and correspondences which we cannot now foresee.

The story of Joseph is not only a picture of Christ's exaltation, but is to us the pledge that the trials we endure for Christ "are achieving for us an eternal glory that far outweighs them all" (2 Corinthians 4:17). In a little while the trials of the present will be exchanged for glories and enjoyments which will make us ashamed that we ever murmured or shrank in the brief ordeal that was only God's beneficent school to educate us for our kingdom. This is the chief lesson of Joseph's life, to teach us the outcome of sorrow, innocently, bravely and triumphantly endured, according to the will of God. It cannot harm us, and the recompense is beyond our highest thought.

An ancient monarch found on ascending to the throne from which a usurper had long excluded him, that one of his faithful adherents was lying in a prison because he had dared to dispute the tyrant's claim and had been true to his exiled master through years of bondage. The victorious king commanded the noble captain to be brought into his presence and the chains struck from his limbs. He then ordered an attendant to weigh them in his sight and then bring from the palace treasuries bag after bag of gold and weigh them on the same scales. Then turning to his faithful friend, he said: "You have worn these chains for me, now you will have their weight in gold. You have languished in a prison for me, now you will have a palace, and all your sufferings will be rewarded by their exact equivalent in riches and honor."

And so for us, "Here is a trustworthy saying: If we died with him, we will also live with him; if we endure, we will also reign with him" (2 Timothy 2:11).

2. Grace Displayed in His Life and Character

Higher far than all Joseph's glory, is the

glorious fact that he used it only for others. The crown of Joseph's character, like his greater Antitype, is love. He stands forever as the highest type of Jesus, our suffering, forgiving brother, and our gracious Lord.

a. We see the beneficence of Joseph's spirit in his kindness, even in his humiliation, to those about him. He ministered to his suffering fellow prisoners. And so Christ went about continually doing good. Likewise, all who are like Christ will live to use every station as an opportunity of service, and leave behind them even in the vilest and meanest place, only memorials of blessing.

b. We see, next, Joseph's graciousness in the use he made of his exalted power. Not for himself did he hold the scepter of Egypt, but for the people he served and saved. The abundance that came to his care was simply regarded as a trust for others and husbanded for the time of their need. So Christ has been exalted to the right hand of power, not for His own selfish magnificence and enjoyment, but that He might be a Prince and a Savior. So He has received all the fullness of the Father that He might give it to the race for which He died. His heavenly life is as unselfish as His earthly, and if we could behold Him now, we would still see the ministering priest, the girded servant, the gracious and ever-willing benefactor of all who need His help and care. He is not a despot, but a loving, toiling, ever-accessible friend. He is never perplexed, never overwhelmed with any difficult situation, never preoccupied,

but ever ready with open ear and heart and hand
to hear our cry and help our need.

> Therefore, since we have a great high
> priest who has gone through the heavens,
> Jesus the Son of God, let us hold firmly to
> the faith we profess. For we do not have a
> high priest who is unable to sympathize
> with our weaknesses, but we have one who
> has been tempted in every way, just as we
> are—yet was without sin. Let us then ap-
> proach the throne of grace with confidence,
> so that we may receive mercy and find grace
> to help us in our time of need. (Hebrews
> 4:14-16)

Like our exalted and beneficent Master, so must
we also use our place of privilege and blessing for
service and for others. We are trustees and stewards
of the manifold grace of God, and the more fully we
receive, the more fully must we learn that "it is
more blessed to give than to receive" (Acts 20:35),
and that the very condition of keeping our blessing
is that we will be a blessing.

A selfish Christian is as inconsistent and impossible as a selfish Christ. We, too, are come to our
kingdom for such a time as this. Years of famine
are coming to the souls around us. In a little
while they will be perishing for lack of eternal
bread. They need our prayers, our help. And although they may not know it now as we do, yet
the day is coming when they will reap the bless-

ings of our faith and our foresight. Let us be true to our trust and thus worthy to stand with Joseph and his greater master, as the dispensers of God's blessings to a dying world.

c. The preeminent picture of Christ's heart is seen in Joseph's relation to his brethren, and his wise and tender, forgiving love. In the wronged and injured brother we see the Savior, and His rejection by those for whom He died. In the long years of indifference and forgetfulness that followed, we behold a picture of the patience that waits while men go on in callousness and hardness of heart. In the troubles that at last overtook them and brought them unconsciously to their injured brother for help, we see how God at length compels the obdurate heart by bitter trials to come to Him, even though it may not yet know Him. In the position of those brothers at the feet of Joseph, unknowing, yet not unknown, we see the sinner whom Christ is drawing to Himself, but who yet does not even know that He is drawing, but is just driving on in some blind course of desperate heedlessness. In the wise and even stern discipline through which Joseph gradually brought them to reflection and the recollection of their sin, and awakened in them the slumbering voice of conscience, we see the exquisite process through which the Holy Spirit convicts the hardened heart of the sinner, and lets its own memories and convictions gently prepare it to receive His mercy. In the deep tenderness that Joseph held in check through all this long ordeal, we see the love that Christ often hides under His sternest discipline and longs to pour out upon us when we are ready to receive it.

At length the hour of reconciliation came. And as in our case, so it began with Joseph, and not with the guilty brothers. God is the first to meet us in reconciliation. It is His love that awakens our trust, and His grace that quickens our heart into grace. How fully Joseph forgives. How tenderly he meets the men that had so pitilessly sacrificed him. How generously he insists that they will forget and forgive themselves. How he tries to banish every painful memory. How he receives them to his very heart and home, and feasts with them in the absence of all other guests. And how royally he provides for them and theirs, sharing with them his wealth and glory, and sending for them to dwell with him amid the abundance of the land and in its fairest region.

All this is infinitely more realized in the love of Jesus, who has been more cruelly wronged. He draws with wiser, tenderer influences of love and power. He it is who says, "I will heal their waywardness and love them freely, for my anger has turned away from them" (Hosea 14:4). Not only does He forgive, but He forgets. Not only does He save from wrath, but He receives us to His friendship, feasts us at His table, feeds us with His own very life, shares with us His riches and glory and takes us to be with Him where He is in all the riches of His kingdom and in-heritance.

As we have already suggested, this will receive a literal fulfillment by and by in the actual seed of Jacob, the literal brethren of Jesus. But it is also fulfilled in the forgiveness and reconciliation of every heart that has learned to know Him as a "friend who sticks closer than a brother" (Proverbs 18:24). Have we learned to know Him by this tender name and this exquisite type? Will we realize with a sweetness unknown before, and reflect upon others, in our turn, like Him, the meaning of these lines?

Yes, for me, for me He careth,
    With a brother's tender care;
Yes, with me, with me He shareth
    Every burden, every fear.

Yes, o'er me, o'er me He watcheth,
    Ceaselessly watcheth night and day;
Yes, e'en me, e'en me he snatcheth
    From the perils of the way.

Yes, in me, in me He dwelleth—
    I in Him, and He in me;
And my empty soul He filleth,
    Here and through eternity.

CHAPTER 9

Emblems from the Life of Moses

And beginning with Moses and all the Prophets, he explained to them what was said in all the Scriptures concerning himself. (Luke 24:27)

This is that Moses who told the Israelites, "God will send you a prophet like me from your own people." He was in the assembly in the desert, with the angel who spoke to him on Mount Sinai, and with our fathers; and he received living words to pass on to us. (Acts 7:37)

We have seen that the first book of the Bible is almost a table of contents of all that was to follow. And that the germ truths of the whole system of redemption are there made living in the personal characters and the symbolic figures that God gave in a series of object lessons to the infant class of His Church. In the book of Exodus the vision grows more vivid, though not less spiritual, and not less Christlike.

The Ark on the Nile

The first that we call attention to is the ark of faith, as we may call it—that little vessel to which a Jewish mother entrusted all her hopes and all the hopes of her people in that hour of strange and terrible extremity. Out of this ark God brought, through His chosen servant, the hope and deliverer of the Church. This picture of Moses and his rescue is the real parable of the whole story of the book of Exodus, and all that it means; namely, the work of redemption.

The word Exodus means "taken out," and the word Moses means "drawn out." And so the Exodus tells how the children of Israel were taken out of Egypt, and thus how we are taken out of the Egypt of sin in like manner. Moses is the figure of their deliverance and ours. Thus his name became expressive of the whole story of the Exodus. He, too, was condemned to die by the harsh decree of the cruel Pharaoh, and he was laid on the altar of death by his mother's trembling hands. He was given up to die, and to her was as really dead, almost as though he had been taken out of her arms and buried. Then he came back to her as much from the dead as Isaac came back to his father. Thus he becomes the symbol of death and resurrection. There is a trial in front of every blessing. There is a cross everywhere, and there is a crown on the other side. Only in the life of faith can we enter into the mystery of

God's working. Little Moses must die and come back to his people, as Christ must be crucified and raised again. And your life must be laid on the altar if you are to come up in resurrection power. So the story of Moses is the parable of resurrection, redemption and the Christian life.

And in handing over that which is so dear to us, there must be faith. We cannot do it unless we trust God. That mother could not have put her cherished one on the waters of the Nile if she had not thought that God's hand was under him and God's power was going to deliver him. It is really a question whether Abraham could have yielded up Isaac as he did, if he had not had faith. It glorifies that act to be told that Abraham believed Isaac would somehow be given back, even from death. It was the faith that made it possible to go through the death. It was the joy that was set before him that enabled Jesus to endure the cross and despise the shame. And so God does not take any of us as blind sacrifices or put us to death in a sort of brutal and hopeless surrender. Rather, He gives us the blessed consciousness that we are in the hands of infinite love, and that, though we may not see how, yet God has for us nothing but blessing and an outcome of mightier joy and service and issues that will reach out through eternity for His glory and for the good of others. So it was here. Little Moses, kept in her home, would have perished. Little Moses, on the Nile, is still alive in his work, and has become the leader of faith for the millions that have followed in his footsteps. And so, the clinging hands that would hold back what God is calling you to give Him, are cruel, foolish hands. Your true life and their true life must ever lie in the example of this ancient mother. Just place all at His blessed feet, and all eternity will unfold to you an hundred-fold.

Again, not only do we see faith here, but we see God's providence that takes the things that we cannot keep, and guards the things for which we cannot care. We are not walking in the dark. There are eyes above us, and around us, and on every side, that never sleep. God can take the very things that you are most afraid of. God can take the very things that are breaking your heart. God can take the very things that seem to be your enemies, and make them the very occasions of your deliverance and the instruments of your highest blessing.

Poor Jochebed was perhaps haunted with the fear of the cruel Pharaoh and his daughter. But she lived to see them the instruments of blessing. The very thing that seemed to condemn her child to death made him the child of a king. The hard fortune by which he was taken from her arms was the doorway by which he was given back. And the very river to which she consigned him, and by which it seemed she was putting him in a watery grave, carried him on the voyage by which he passed from being a Hebrew captive to being the lawgiver of the world. The very things that are hard to suffer become the scaffolding for building

God's temple, without which He could not have fulfilled His purpose.

This is also true in the story of Joseph. He had to go into the dungeon to be a prince. And Moses had to be decreed to death, to be cast into the waters, to be saved, and to become the instrument of God to save these people. Oh, let us trust that inscrutable Providence, which is so full of mystery to many, and which hides, behind His trials and discipline, plans and purposes of love and wisdom. Through this little floating vessel, let us learn the secret of self-renunciation. Let us learn the secret of trust. Let our trembling hands place all that is dear into His infinite arms, and ever keep it there. And with wondering hearts we, too, will know how wise, how strong is His hand.

The Burning Bush

The second emblem in the book of Exodus is the fire of the wilderness, the burning bush.

> There the angel of the LORD appeared to him in flames of fire from within a bush. Moses saw that though the bush was on fire it did not burn up. So Moses thought, "I will go over and see this strange sight—why the bush does not burn up."
>
> When the LORD saw that he had gone over to look, God called to him from within the bush, "Moses! Moses!"
>
> And Moses said, "Here I am."
>
> "Do not come any closer," God said.

"Take off your sandals, for the place where you are standing is holy ground." Then he said, "I am the God of your father, the God of Abraham, the God of Isaac and the God of Jacob." At this, Moses hid his face, because he was afraid to look at God.

The LORD said, "I have indeed seen the misery of my people in Egypt. I have heard them crying out because of their slave drivers, and I am concerned about their suffering. So I have come down to rescue them from the hand of the Egyptians and to bring them up out of that land into a good and spacious land, a land flowing with milk and honey—the home of the Canaanites, Hittites, Amorites, Perizzites, Hivites and Jebusites. And now the cry of the Israelites has reached me, and I have seen the way the Egyptians are oppressing them. So now, go. I am sending you to Pharaoh to bring my people the Israelites out of Egypt." (Exodus 3:2-10)

Here we see the story of Egypt again represented in symbol, just as it was in the waters of the Nile. Only the figure here is not water, but fire. It grows more intense, more terrible. And so God's image to us of trial and of trouble is both water and fire, and He has given us a promise for both.

When you pass through the waters,
    I will be with you;

and when you pass through the rivers,
  they will not sweep over you.
When you walk through the fire,
  you will not be burned;
  the flames will not set you ablaze.
For I am the LORD, your God,
  the Holy One of Israel, your Savior.
    (Isaiah 43:2-3)

And so, while the waters of the Nile tell of the engulfing tribulation, the burning bush tells of the tribulations which seem to be a consuming fire.

The bush referred to here was a little stunted shrub that still grows in the wilderness of that country. It was not a palm tree. It was not a beautiful bush full of blossoms. It was a fitting type of these and of the Church of God, although a despised little thing. And so it is with our Christ life: a root out of a dry ground, like the heath in the desert—to the eye of man, not only obscure, but burning with fiery trial.

Fire represents here what had been represented to Abraham in the smoking furnace of his vision. It represents the fiery trials of our lives, the things that burn down deep into the very fibers of our being, the flames that penetrate and seem to become the very substance of our soul. Fire is strangely intense and intrinsic. It goes into the very substance of things. It somehow blends with every particle of the thing it touches.

Somehow, there are trials that penetrate so that

some of us do not know a moment of life without them, nor a spot that does not hold them. There are seasons of trial—what is called, in the Bible, "the day of evil." There are the physical trials, the social and domestic trials, and the things that grieve the tenderest sensibilities and break the loving, sympathizing heart. There are the trials of uncongenial surroundings and unfavorable circumstances. There are the severer trials that come to minds more sensitive, to the minds that have more points of contact with what hurts. The higher the nature the higher the joy, and the greater the avenues of pain that can come. And then there are the deeper trials that come as we pass into the hands of God, as we pass from the psychical and intellectual nature. Peter calls them "the painful trial you are suffering" (1 Peter 4:12). When it first comes, we shrink back from its unnatural and fearful breath, and we say: "Oh, this cannot be from the hand of a loving Father. This cannot be necessary for me."

Oh, the fearfulness of the struggle! The strange, sulphurous smell that comes from its exhalations, and so sickens and withers, sometimes, our spiritual sensibilities! And then the pains and sufferings that come from God's own hand. When He sits as a refiner and purifier of silver (Malachi 3:3), when He lets it burn, and burn, and burn, and burn in, until it seems that we must be burned to ashes, and we are indeed at last burned to ashes. "For our 'God is a consuming fire' " (Hebrews 12:29).

The Holy Spirit will baptize you with fire. This fire sometimes means suffering in your deeper spiritual being, until your soul becomes partaker of the virtue of God. But then all the fires cannot consume you. I know that some of you can understand this. This is one of the things that does not need philosophy to explain. Christ knew it, and He talks to us as a suffering people. The Bible asserts that we are the children of affliction. Though trial does not spring from the ground or from the clouds, yet man is born to it as the sparks fly upward. But, blessed be His name, if you are God's workmanship, the bush burns, but is not consumed. If one branch of God's little shrub is reduced, or calcined by that little flame, it does not harm anything that is real. They walk through the midst of the fire, without the smell of the flame on their garments. They come forth, set free from its vehemence and fury, set free from the very chains that had been on their limbs when they entered the furnace. God tells us that trouble cannot harm us if we are His. He was showing Moses that His people could not be destroyed by these persecutions, for, the more they were persecuted, the more they grew and multiplied. Our troubles have not harmed us, if we are the Lord's. We will suffer no loss through them.

But we must get the victory through faith. We must get above the billowing wave or it will sink us. The moment you cease to fear it, that moment it ceases to harm you. "The rivers will not sweep over you," He says, "The flames will not set you ablaze" (see Isaiah 43:2). The flames will burn something, but nothing that is divine. God must burn all else someday, and it is better now. The fire will try men's souls to see what they are, and where there is hay or stubble, it will burn like tinder, in the last day. Is it not better now? There are things in you that will burn, but they are not divine things. God wants you to be made free from everything that would consume.

I take a piece of paper and put it in the gas jet, and how quickly it burns up! But I can keep a piece of gold there all day, and yet it is not burned. It may melt, but it is all there. It is indestructible. And so God wants to take out of you and me that which is perishable. "Oh," let us say, "anything in me that will not stand in that day, let it go, and give me that which will stand." If the faith withers, maybe it was not faith. And if the song dies out, maybe it was only an earthly song. Possibly God is letting your natural strength wither, that you may take the strength of God. He is letting your old powers shrink, that you may get rooted in the rock. That which burns out is transient and earthly, and God is burning it out that you may get something better. You know that He is burning out the dross of sin. Are you willing for Him to do this?

I have no doubt that there was some way in which the children of Israel were being prepared for their future by their sufferings. We may not understand it, but God does. And so the peaceable fruits will come out of our trials.

Is it not wonderful that here the very figure that is used to express the suffering, the very emblem of their terrible furnace of affliction, is the type of Christ Himself? The burning flame is God's most ancient emblem of His own image, and the one that shines preeminently above all other symbols among His ancient people. In Eden He appeared as the fiery Shekinah. And preceding, or following, the children of Israel in their journeying, was the pillar of cloud and fire. So the symbol of God throughout the Old Testament was fire. In the tabernacle the Spirit of God was represented by the flame above the ark. At Mount Sinai He came down in the fire and in the lightning. When He came to judge, He came in fire. So, again, when Elijah called on God on Mount Carmel, He answered by fire. When the Holy Spirit came, we are told in the book of Acts that cloven tongues of fire sat upon each of the disciples. Thus fire was the special enrobing of the divine form. It tells not only of our sorrow, but of Him who comes to us in our sorrow.

As we look at the licking tongues of flame and think of its consuming power, suddenly it becomes transformed, and over its glowing figure we behold the name of God and read these words: "I AM WHO I AM" (Exodus 3:14). And so this figure of the burning bush not only represents the suffering Church, but also God in the midst of His people, pervading them with His life, and thus making them indestructible in the midst of trials and temptations, sustained and upheld by His own indwelling and His mighty all-sufficiency.

Dear friend, do you know this indwelling fire? Is it not the God of judgment who is a consuming fire? The language of Paul is: "Our 'God is a consuming fire' " (Hebrews 12:29). The God who comes to us, the God whom we love to have come to us. Has He come to us as a fire? Has He come to consume the perishable and the corruptible, the sinful and the narrow? Has He burned out of you the foolishness, the sinfulness, the weakness and the selfishness? Will you let Him?

This is a wholesome fire; it is a blessed fire. The thing you want consumed is a wilderness of woods and swamp. When a fire starts in a swamp, how quickly the wild things get out. How the serpents hiss and flee, and how everything is cleansed. God wants to burn the nest of scorpions out of your heart. Ask Him to let the fire in. If you have anything wrong in your heart, ask Him to come and consume it. There are things in your heart that you want burned out. You want it as empty as a vessel that has been through the flames. We need not only to be washed out, but to be burned out, if we would be pure vessels fit for the Master's use. Ask Him to send the fire, and receive it as the fire of love. Oh, for the divine love that endures all things, that hopes all things, that never fails (1 Corinthians 13:7-8). Let it burn on and on and never cease—the unquenchable fire of God in the heart. Then will it be what the fire is in the wheels of human industry, moving the machinery of life. He will baptize you with the Holy Spirit and with fire, a glowing thing—little and obscure, but a wonder to earth and heaven, alive with light and glory and purity. It is nothing in yourself, but, like wire charged with electric fire so that a man would not dare touch it, it is so alive.

So you, though little and lowly, may be fiery channels to touch other lives and make them yield to Him. Let us realize that the dispensation of today is as supernatural as that of Pentecost. It was the Holy Spirit that was in the shrub. He is as present here, and He can make of you all you will let Him.

The Rod of Moses

The third emblem we will look at is the rod referred to in the fourth chapter of Exodus. Moses said: "What if they do not believe me or listen to me and say, 'The LORD did not appear to you'?" (Exodus 4:1).

God did not say to him, "I am going to give you some great sign." But He said, " 'What is that in your hand?' 'A staff,' he replied" (4:2). That was God's sign to Moses that God was to be with him. When the Lord wants to give you a sign to the world that He is in you, He is not going to do it by an astonishing emblem. He is going to say to you: "What is that in your hand?" He is going to take the most common thing in your life and make it mighty in His service. He is going to prove that His presence is in you, and that He is going to work with your nothingness and simplicity. The very thing of all on which the commission of Moses rested was the simplest and smallest and weakest thing about him. That little shepherd's crook, the little thorn bush he had cut in the desert was to be the weapon with which he was to go to Pharaoh and challenge his power, and open a pathway for God's redeemed people to walk through the sea on dry land, and bring the cloud of glory to lead as they marched forth. That little rod, the very emblem of insignificance and weakness, was the emblem of God's power and the token of His presence.

Beloved, do you want to know whether God is in your heart, whether God is really all in all? Then, what are you doing with that in your hand? What is God making out of your common life? And is God using the little things about you, your very weakness? What has God made out of your rod? That is what it all means. It does not mean that you are to get into an ideal state, and when you are particularly strong and adapted to your work, God is going to use you. God is going to start now. He wants to take you today. And the very thing He wants to baptize with the Holy Spirit is not something that you hope to have by the spring or autumn, but what you have got this morning or evening. The very trial in your life from which you want deliverance, He wants to take now and make it the opportunity of your service and then you can be at God's disposal. The very work in your hand He wants to come into now and make a token of His power. The very thing you are trying to get over and make satisfactory to yourself, He wants surrendered as it is. God meets you with that which is in your hand, and He wants to use you with what you have, and what you are, and then prepare you for whatever He has in reserve for you in His purpose and wisdom.

So we find all through the Bible that God takes people in the place He finds them and in the relations His providence has already given them, and uses them. So not only with Moses but a score of others, God has taken their occupation, and made them illustrious examples of His power. He came to Joshua and used him for what he was fitted—a soldier. He came to Deborah and used her as a woman. He came to Miriam and said, "What do you have?" "A tambourine," she answered, and He used her to sing the song of Moses and the Lamb. He came to Hannah—she had a mother's heart—and He took that, and out of it came Samuel and his service. He came to Samson, and He did not wait for anything better than an old skeleton bone—that was enough. He came to David, the shepherd boy, and made him a king before he had any military training or knew anything of a courtier's life. And so, at a later period, He took Paul, the tentmaker, and William Carey at his bench, and David Livingstone at his shuttle, a missionary before he ever saw Africa.

And so He takes you. You do not need to be

anything better than the burning bush. That is not perhaps all He will yet use. If He will give you culture, He will use that when it is in your hand. But He will not use you until you use what you have. If the fire is not burning in your heart, do not put on any more green wood. What are you doing today? What are you letting God do?

It was not Moses who did it—it was God. Moses tried to do it forty years before, but God would not have any of his trying. Moses had put himself in the front and taken his sword and killed an Egyptian and hidden him in the sand. Then he said, "That is the way I am going to treat all who misuse my brethren." But the next day he was glad to run away and hide from the consequences of his impulsiveness. God would not have him then. But for forty years He slowly tempered him. He steeped him in the waters of patient trial. He humbled him so that now He had to goad him and push him out. He said: "I cannot speak, Lord; send anybody, but do not send me." When God got him there, reduced to the smallest of proportions, the weakest of all the men who ever lived, He said: "You are ready for work. Now, Moses, I am going to take that rod and with it break the arms of Pharaoh, and open the way for My people, and bring waters from the desert rock and make you an instrument of power."

Is it not the New Testament lesson? "God chose the foolish things of the world to shame the wise; God chose the weak things of the world to shame the strong. He chose the lowly things of this world and the despised things—and the things that are not—to nullify the things that are, so that no one may boast before him" (1 Corinthians 1:27-29). He wants only to have our nothingness. But we must have Him.

And so as the closing lesson we want to learn that back of the story of the burning bush and the rod there is another fact that overshadows all, transcends all—written in the sky, written on the sacred page, written henceforth on Moses' heart, and, I hope, on ours—the mighty name that God pronounces for the first time, "I AM." (Exodus 3:14). "I AM WHO I AM" (3:14).

"Lord, how will they know? How will I get them to accept me?"

"Certainly, I will be with you. I AM WHO I AM. You! Why you have not anything to do, but just to go. But I AM, and you are not. You are a little shrub. I am the fire that burns in it. No man dare touch it any more than he dare touch that charged wire to harm it. What does it matter about the brush, if the right painter wields it? What does it matter about the harp—if the right musician plays it he can bring music out of a broken string. And so, I AM! And if you want anything more, I AM WHO I AM. It is just I AM . . . I AM . . . I AM."

It is the Personal One—the One we have been learning to receive. Try to get out of His way and make room for Him to come in. Over against our nothingness, over against all we fear or desire on earth or in heaven, let us put "I AM."

He keeps on saying it through the New Testament. He says it to His disciples on the stormy sea. He says it to you, "It is I. Don't be afraid." And he is hovering over us between earth and heaven—and again, about to ascend, He speaks to His disciples, saying, "All authority in heaven and on earth has been given to me. . . . And surely I am with you always, to the very end of the age" (Matthew 28:18, 20). It still is "I AM."

And again, in the last book, in the Apocalypse, He adds, "I am the Living One; I was dead, and behold I am alive for ever and ever!" (Revelation 1:18).

This is the secret of power. It is not merely ceasing from yourself, but it is seeing Him. It is not merely dying, but it is letting Him live. It is not merely saying, I am not sufficient to think anything of myself, but it is putting out your hands and saying, "But our competence comes from God" (2 Corinthians 3:5). "Having nothing"—it would kill us if we stopped there—"and yet possessing everything" (6:10).

That is the reason He wants you to get off the old raft, that you may get on the ship of power and all-sufficiency. That is the reason He wants you to let go of your old miserable way and be carried by the train of His almighty power. How many of us have stopped with the discouragements, the nothingness. Now, beloved, take hold of His strength. For everything you have let go there is a hundredfold—take it. Have you done so? Come, that God may fill your life. Place all that you have at His feet, and before the sun goes down you will triumph there. Moses and Jehovah, the rod is enough, only let God wield it.

Somebody wanted once to see the sword of Richard Coeur de Lion—I think it was Saladin the Saracen—and when he saw it he said, "Why, that is not half as good a sword as mine. That is nothing but a cleaver. Look at my sword." And he took out the burnished blade and doubled it until the point touched the hilt. "Look, it is elastic, and this blade is like a razor."

The man quietly looked at him, and then said, "Saladin, it is not the sword of Richard, it is the arm of Richard that wields it, that makes it what it is."

Oh, beloved, we are enough, you are enough, if we will only let Him hide us in His shadow and uphold us with His hand. "[I am he] who holds the seven stars in his right hand," He says (Revelation 2:1). Take His great name today. Fill up the blank in your own covenant, and write after that, "I am! I am joy. I am power. I am love. I am faith. I am providence. I am in the future and in the past. I am Jesus. I am yours. I am in you. I am your faith, and your power, and your salvation. Take Me bodily, and own Me utterly, for I am your God. You are not your own, I am not My own, but yours. I am yours and you are Mine." Amen.

CHAPTER 10

Emblems from Israel's Bondage and Redemption

There are numerous symbols we can find in the story of Israel's bondage and redemption.

The Brick Fields of Egypt

They made their lives bitter with hard labor in brick and mortar and with all kinds of work in the fields; in all their hard labor the Egyptians used them ruthlessly. (Exodus 1:14)

That same day Pharaoh gave this order to the slave drivers and foremen in charge of the people: "You are no longer to supply the people with straw for making bricks; let them go and gather their own straw. But require them to make the same number of bricks as before; don't reduce the quota." (5:6-8)

So the people scattered all over Egypt to gather stubble to use for straw. The slave drivers kept pressing them, saying, "Complete the work required of you for each day, just as when you had straw." The Israelite foremen appointed by Pharaoh's slave drivers were beaten and were asked, "Why haven't you met your quota of bricks yesterday or today, as before?"

Then the Israelite foremen went and appealed to Pharaoh: "Why have you treated your servants this way? Your servants are given no straw, yet we are told, 'Make bricks!' Your servants are being beaten, but the fault is with your own people." (5:12-16)

The Israelite foremen realized they were in trouble when they were told, "You are not to reduce the number of bricks required of you for each day." (5:19)

This is the picture which God has given us of the bitter bondage of His ancient people, which is a type of the rigid slavery of sin and Satan.

The land which had been their asylum in the beginning had become to them an iron furnace and a place of oppression.

Through all the succeeding centuries the language, "I am the LORD your God, who brought you out of Egypt, out of the land of slavery" (20:2), has been the strongest and most vivid picture of our redemption from the power of Satan and this present evil world.

To us, as to them, it began with a scene of innocence and blessing. But soon another king arose over our once holy and happy Eden, and the prince of this world holds his captives in slavery more perfect and a servitude more debasing than Pharaoh or Israel ever knew.

The brick fields of Zoan are fitting emblems of some of its rigors. The very material of which the brick is made suggests the idea of the earthly and perishable. The symbol of God's enduring work is not brick but stone. The heavenly house is founded upon a rock, and its separate materials are living stones. But the houses of Egypt and Babylon are built of clay and symbolize the transitory and earthly character and issue of all that pertains to this evil world.

The poor votary of Mammon is spending all his strength to build a house which will crumble, like himself, into dust when a few more years will have passed away.

The aggravation of this bondage, however, was that the oppressor demanded the severest tasks, without even supplying materials or resources. This is exactly what Satan does with all his victims—demands that they make brick without straw.

He is the great master of an evil conscience. He loves to lay upon the troubled heart the yoke of the law, quite as well as he does to break its obligations. One of his favorite methods of crushing his victims is to demand of them an impossible righteousness, and then accuse them and condemn them and drive them to despair because they have not fulfilled it, although he knows that they are wholly unable to do so.

How dreadful is the bondage of a soul conscious of its sin and shortcoming. It is constantly desiring to do better, and indeed, rushing into a thousand resolves and purposes of right doing, and yet sinking deeper into the captivity of corruption, beaten for every failure with the cruel rod of an accusing conscience and a remorseful despair. How different His gentle sway, who commands nothing without also giving the power to fulfill it, and who says to the weary and sin-trodden world,

> Come to me, all you who are weary and burdened, and I will give you rest. Take my yoke upon you and learn from me, for I am gentle and humble in heart, and you will find rest for your souls. For my yoke is easy and my burden is light. (Matthew 11:28-30)

The figure reaches its climax when it is added that the wages of this pitiless service was literally, death. The cruel decree not only demanded that the race should be crushed and prostrated by these severe exactions, but also that it should be ultimately extinguished, by the consignment to a cruel fate of every male child.

So our hard master not only seeks our service, but has determined upon our utter destruction.

Nothing less than the blood of our soul will ever satisfy his fiendish hate and malignity. He is not satisfied with our physical death, but his sting strikes us with an eternal wound and smites with an eternal death. What fools men are! They are building what they think are their treasure cities. But like the piles of ancient Rameses and Python they pass into the hands of others, and the wretched toilers go down to an eternal grave. "For the wages of sin is death, but the gift of God is eternal life in Christ Jesus our Lord" (Romans 6:23).

This cruel bondage is as unrelenting as it is severe. Pharaoh had no intention of letting his captives go. He made a little compromise and consented that they should go for a few days into the wilderness to worship God; but they must not go very far away. In no case must they go out of Egypt. And even if they go, they must leave their cattle and their children as hostages (Exodus 8, 9). So the world holds men. It has no objections to a moderate amount of religion, so long as it does not separate us from the world or lead us very far from its practices and spirit. Like Pharaoh it always insists on holding our family and our property. Where Satan has not all the hearts, he generally controls a large part of the capital, even of the professed people of God. Parents who themselves would not dream of indulging in doubtful association and pleasures, allow their children unrestrained liberty in the enjoyment of the world.

It is a blessing when God makes the bondage so bitter that His people awake to the realization of its meaning and cry like Israel of old for deliverance. Like them the cry will be met, not only by the Lord's mercy, but by the enhanced severity of their trials. The nearer the hour of deliverance, the more terrific was the heat of the iron furnace. And so it is, often, that in the very depths of despair the morning breaks and the deliverer comes to us. "When the tale of bricks is double, then comes Moses," is the beautiful proverb already referred to, in which the sad story of Israel crystallizes its hope. Many a soul has found it true in the experience of salvation or providential deliverance.

Let us stop and ask ourselves what all this means for us. Are we in the brick fields of Egypt, or in the free and happy tents of the redeemed? Are we building the house of sand that will crumble into decay and ruin in a little while? Or are we building not only on the rock, but also of the precious, indestructible materials of gold, silver, and precious stones, which will not only stand the test, but shine the brighter in the flames of the final day?

Are we serving that cruel master, the world, who deceives us by his fair promises and makes us think we are building palaces for ourselves, and then snatches them from the crumbling fingers that can hold them no longer, and who repeats the story of the world's deceiving promises in the lives that come after us?

Are we the wretched slaves of a tyrant who is not only using all our strength for his own selfish ends, but who is slowly and inevitably crushing us to an eternal death; but has determined not only to destroy our lives, but to devour our immortal souls? Are we under the bondage of an evil conscience, and a law that can no longer save or sanctify? Are we wasting our lives and spending our strength for nothing in a futile endeavor to keep our resolutions and reform our lives, overcome our passions, and fulfill the demands of that law, but with every failure are sinking deeper into helplessness and despair?

Blessed be God! For us the hour of redemption draws near. The rigors of our bondage are but the last frantic, convulsive efforts of our tyrant to hold us. The Great Deliverer has come "to bind up the broken-hearted, to proclaim freedom for the captives and release from darkness for the prisoners" (Isaiah 61:1), to rescue us "from the dominion of darkness and [bring] us into the kingdom of the Son he loves" (Colossians 1:13).

Only let us recognize our true condition. Let us take His side against our oppressor. Let us not, like them, refuse Moses when he comes to set us free. Let us lift up our cry to heaven, and the answer is already spoken.

And now the cry of the Israelites has reached me, and I have seen the way the Egyptians are oppressing them. (Exodus 3:9)

I have indeed seen the misery of my people in Egypt. I have heard them crying out because of their slave drivers, and I am concerned about their suffering. So I have come down to rescue them. (3:7)

The Ten Plagues

The first stage of the deliverance of Israel was the judgment of God upon their oppressors. The ten plagues of Egypt are types of the dealings of God with our spiritual adversaries in the great work of redemption, both in its inception and final consummation.

We have already seen the principle of salvation by destruction vividly illustrated in the story of the deluge, where Noah and his family were saved by water. The destruction of Pharaoh is a similar illustration of the same principle. The ten plagues of Egypt were directed not only against the persons and property of the king and nation, but more especially against the devil gods and deified naturalism of the land. "I will bring judgment," God says, "on all the gods of Egypt" (12:12).

The ten successive plagues that filled the river with blood and the land with swarms of frogs, flies and locusts and smote the cattle with disease, the fields with hail and fire, the sky with darkness, and all the homes of Egypt with death were not only tokens of God's displeasure against the wicked tyrant and the corrupt people. They were a direct and fatal blow at the dragonhead of him who was the real lord of Egypt—the prince of the powers of the air, the ruler of earth's ungodly nations, and the god of this world.

The Nile, the flocks, the beetles, the cattle, the sun, and the king himself, were all representatives of the divine principle and objects of idolatrous worship. They were all in turn smitten in helpless judgment by the hand of heaven, that Egypt might know that they were but the mockeries of a false religion and the counterfeits of the true God, who was about to magnify Himself in the redemption and history of His chosen people.

These plagues that foreshadowed the judgments that began to fall upon the head of Satan, even in the earthly ministry of the Lord Jesus, are to reach their culmination in the plagues of judgment of the last day.

The first three of these fell alike both on Israel and the Egyptians, implying that to a certain extent even the people of God share in the sufferings and retributions which sin has brought upon the earth. But the last seven were exclusively confined to the Egyptians and seem to contain a prophecy, or at least a prefiguring shadow, of the seven last plagues, which in a little while are to fill up the cup of earth's calamities and immediately precede the personal advent of the Lord Jesus Christ (Revelation 16).

The doom of Pharaoh in the Red Sea is the type of the final overthrow of Satan and his earthly viceregents at the opening of Christ's millennial reign. Not always will right be on the scaffold and wrong upon the throne. "He who is coming will come and will not delay" (Hebrews 10:37). "Evil men and impostors will go from bad to worse" (2 Timothy 3:13). But there is an end to wickedness, and "The scepter of the wicked will not remain over the land allotted to the righteous" (Psalm 125:3).

The chain is forged and the sword is whetted which are to find and smite the tyrant and oppressor of the ages. Soon the cry will rise again: "The accuser of our brothers, . . . has been hurled down. . . . Rejoice, you heavens and you who dwell in them" (Revelation 12:10, 12). "Hallelujah! For our Lord God Almighty reigns" (19:6). As on the farther shore of the Egyptian sea they sang the song of Moses, they will finish the refrain in a grander chorus and sing the song of Moses and the song of the Lamb before the sea of glass, saying,

> Great and marvelous are your deeds,
>   Lord God Almighty.
> Just and true are your ways,
>   King of the ages.
> Who will not fear you, O Lord,
>   and bring glory to your name?
> For you alone are holy.
> All nations will come
>   and worship before you,
> for your righteous acts have been revealed.
>   (15:3-4)

The Paschal Lamb

The LORD said to Moses and Aaron in Egypt, "This month is to be for you the first month, the first month of your year. . . . on the tenth day of this month each man is to take a lamb for his family, one for each household. If any household is too small for a whole lamb, they must share one with their nearest neighbor, having taken into account the number of people there are. . . . The animals you choose must be year-old males without defect. . . . Take care of them until the fourteenth day of the month, when all the people of the community of Israel must slaughter them at twilight. Then they are to take some of the blood and put it on the sides and tops of the doorframes of the houses where they eat the lambs. That same night they are to eat the meat roasted over the fire, along with bitter herbs, and bread made without yeast. . . . This is how you are to eat it: with your cloak tucked into your belt, your sandals on your feet and your staff in your hand. Eat it in haste; it is the LORD's Passover.

"On that same night I will pass through Egypt and strike down every firstborn—both men and animals—and I will bring judgment on all the gods of Egypt. I am the LORD. The blood will be a sign for you on the houses where you are; and when I see the blood, I will pass over you. No destructive plague will touch you when I strike Egypt.

"This is a day you are to commemorate; for the generations to come you shall celebrate it as a festival to the Lord—a lasting ordinance." (Exodus 12:1–14)

Thus did Jehovah mark the starting point of their national history by this crimson token of redemption. So for the Church of the New Testament, and so for every redeemed soul, the beginning of months is the cross of Calvary and the shed and sprinkled blood. The Paschal Lamb was but the summing up in one enduring ordinance of all the sacrificial types which already had been instituted for nearly thirty centuries.

The selection of the lamb on the tenth day of the month and its being kept until the fourteenth, suggest unmistakably the coming of Christ in the fullness of time, and the three and a half years of His public ministry after He was set apart to His redeeming work by His baptism and while waiting for the accomplishment of His sacrifice. The death of the lamb before the whole assembly of the children of Israel reminds us of how He was delivered up by the national council of His own people and formally condemned to death at the hands of the Romans. The very time of its death corresponded exactly with the sacrifice of Calvary. The sprinkled blood expresses our personal application of the merits of His death. The efficacy of that blood in averting the stroke of the avenging angel is fulfilled in the security into which redemption brings us and the complete justification and acceptance of the soul that has found refuge under the precious blood.

The flesh of the lamb reminds us that Christ is not only a substitute for us, but the very substance and subsistence of our spiritual life through His living union and communion with us.

As it was eaten that same night that it was slain, so we must feed on Christ from the moment that we accept Him.

The unleavened bread helps us to remember that our most holy faith leaves no place for indulgence of sin, but requires our turning from all iniquity if we would claim that redeeming blood. And the bitter herbs spell out the story of repentance and contrition in the life of every forgiven soul. This, then, was the ground of their redemption, and this is the purchase of ours.

> In him we have redemption through his blood, the forgiveness of sins, in accordance with the riches of God's grace. (Ephesians 1:7)

> It was not with perishable things such as silver or gold that you were redeemed . . . but with the precious blood of Christ, a lamb without blemish or defect. He was chosen before the creation of the world, but was revealed in these last times for your sake. (1 Peter 1:18-20)

> To him who loves us and has freed us
> from our sins by his blood . . . be glory and
> power for ever and ever! (Revelation 1:5-6)

Have we learned to blend the song of Moses
and the song of the Lamb? Are we resting under
the flesh of the Paschal Lamb? Is our bread unleavened? Are our feet sandaled, our staves in
hand, and our pilgrimage begun? Are you sure
the blood is on the door?

An old Hebrew legend tells us this was the cry
of a little girl that first passover night. "Father,
are you sure?" They looked and found it had
been entrusted to another and neglected. With
eager hands it was quickly sprinkled, and the little heart could rest while waiting for their journey to begin. Oh, if any one who reads these
lines is still in Egypt and under the black wing
of night and judgment, make haste to apply it.
The gentle Lamb stands with bowed head by
your side. For a little longer He offers His
bosom to death and His blood to wash away
your sin. One cry of penitence, one look of
earnest longing, one touch of simple faith, and
you will have passed under the protection of His
death and life. The one will cancel all your guilt.
The other will quicken and keep all your future
life in covenant love and care. And this hour will
be to you the beginning of the months of your
eternal history. It will not be forgotten even
when before the sea of glass you sing the song of
Moses and the Lamb.

Notice most emphatically that the safety of Israel did not depend upon their personal feelings or merits, but on the attitude they took with respect to the lamb and the blood. And so, beloved reader, your eternal future hangs absolutely upon your relation to the Lord Jesus Christ. "Whoever believes in the Son has eternal life, but whoever rejects the Son will not see life, for God's wrath remains on him" (John 3:36). Out from under the blood you are lost, whoever and wherever you may be. Under its sprinkled canopy you are as safe as an angel and as dear to God as His only, well-beloved Son.

The Passage of the Red Sea

The LORD hardened the heart of Pharaoh . . . so that he pursued the Israelites . . . and overtook them as they camped by the sea. . . .

As Pharaoh approached, the Israelites looked up, and there were the Egyptians, marching after them. They were terrified and cried out to the LORD. . . . (Exodus 14:8-10)

Moses answered the people, "Do not be afraid. Stand firm and you will see the deliverance the LORD will bring you today. The Egyptians you see today you will never see again. The LORD will fight for you; you need only to be still."

Then the LORD said to Moses, "Why are you crying out to me? Tell the Israelites to move on. Raise your staff and stretch out your hand over the sea to divide the water so that the Israelites can go through the sea on dry ground." (14:13-16)

Then Moses stretched out his hand over the sea, and all that night the LORD drove the sea back with a strong east wind and turned it into dry land. The waters were divided, and the Israelites went through the sea on dry ground, with a wall of water on their right and on their left.

The Egyptians pursued them, and all Pharaoh's horses and chariots and horsemen followed them into the sea. (14:21-23)

Moses stretched out his hand over the sea, and at daybreak the sea went back to its place. The Egyptians were fleeing toward it, and the LORD swept them into the sea. The water flowed back and covered the chariots and horsemen—the entire army of Pharaoh that had followed the Israelites into the sea. . . .

But the Israelites went through the sea on dry ground, with a wall of water on their right and on their left. That day the LORD saved Israel from the hands of the Egyptians, and Israel saw the Egyptians lying dead on the shore. And when the Israelites saw the great power the LORD displayed against the Egyptians, the people feared the LORD and put their trust in him and in Moses his servant. (14:27–31)

Such is the sublime type of our salvation, repeated afresh in every new and great deliverance which comes in the life of faith. The principles are ever the same. God alone must deliver, and we must let Him, ceasing from our own works, implicitly trusting Him, and fearlessly obeying and following Him. This is the beautiful figure of the commitment of faith, when the soul first comes in trembling fear to Christ for salvation. Pursued by its sins and its bitter adversaries, it sees no way before, and there is no retreat behind. Then comes the blessed word, "Stand firm, and you will see the deliverance the Lord will bring." Our first act must be to cease from our own efforts to save ourselves; the next to keep our eye upon God; and then the third, to go forward, not in the old and restless way of the self-effort, but in simple obedience to His leading and in confidence in His promise. There may seem no pathway but the raging sea, but the soul may commit itself securely to Him, and at once step out into the darkness of the inevitable future, and it will find a pathway for redemption and victory.

So we must act in the great crises of difficulty and danger that meet us along the pathway of life. Our first expressions are usually those of distrust and fear, like poor fleeing Israel. And our greatest danger is that we will become so agitated and active in our wild efforts to save ourselves that God cannot really help us. Therefore His word again is to stand still. We must absolutely stop all our contriving, fretting and rushing hither and thither, and let the Lord take charge.

Next we must get our eyes on Him, and see the salvation of the Lord, and know that He will fight for us. And as we do this we must continue to hold our peace. We must not begin again the outcries of fear or impatience. We must rest in the Lord and wait patiently for Him. Then will come the moment to go forward, and our going will be safe and effectual. There may be no pathway visible. It may be stepping into the cold floods for a moment. But we will find dry land as we advance, and on the farther shore we will have a song such as they only know who have learned to trust in the dark and sing in the night.

> March on then right boldly,
> The sea will divide,
> The pathway made glorious,
> With shoutings victorious,
> We'll join in the chorus,
> The Lord will provide.

The passage of the Red Sea was not only a beautiful symbol of the commitment of faith, but also of death and resurrection. Hence it is called by the Apostle Paul, "baptized into Moses in the cloud and in the sea" (1 Corinthians 10:2). It expresses the radical idea of baptism very vividly; namely, death and resurrection life. It was a seeming grave, as our baptism is. And yet like ours also, only a seeming death, for they found the solid ground beneath their feet. Yet it was really death to their enemies. So as we become united to Christ in His death and resurrection, the only things that die are our spiritual enemies. And on the farther shore we see the Egyptians as helpless corpses, unable to harm us again.

Thus God permits us to bury our sins, our past lives, our old selves, and even the world of Egypt which has enslaved us and debased us. This is the glorious meaning of the cross of Jesus. And all who have really accepted it in its real meaning can sing

I've passed the cross of Calvary;
I'm on the heaven side.

Again, beloved, where do we stand amid these ancient figures of redemption? Have we ceased from our own works and accepted the salvation of the Lord? Have we gone forth in a full committal of faith and begun like them our Christian pilgrimage? Have we died to sin and recognized our guilt as buried in the depths of the sea? Have we died to the spirit of self and the world and left the spirit of Egypt forever behind us? Are we living on the Canaan side of the cross? Have we learned the secret of deliverance in the narrow places of trial through the stillness of faith and the interposition of God? Let us go forth from these meditations with a clearer view of our complete redemption, our line of eternal demarcation and separation from the world, our real resurrection life, and our glorious prospects as we now begin, amid the teachings of these ancient types, our Christian pilgrimage.

The Song of Moses

It only remains to add in conclusion that the song of Moses and of Miriam on the farther side of the Egyptian sea was the keynote of the song of salvation in every redeemed soul. It is the song of deliverance which every visitation of God's providence inspires, and the song of Him in whom all these notes will yet be gathered up amid the choirs of glory.

Have we learned that first song?

> I will praise you, O LORD.
> Although you were angry with me,
> your anger has turned away
>   and you have comforted me.
> Surely God is my salvation;
>   I will trust and not be afraid.
> The LORD, the LORD, is my strength
>   and my song;
>   he has become my salvation."
>   (Isaiah 12:1-2)

Have we learned the song of deliverance, which is first the Berachah song going before the redeemed like the choirs of Jehoshaphat, and then bringing up the rear with praise for accomplished blessing? And will we have our part in that grander chorus where the multitude that no man can number, out of all kindreds and tongues and peoples and nations, will sing and shout, "Salvation belongs to our God, who sits on the throne, and to the Lamb" (Revelation 7:10)?

> Worthy is the Lamb, who was slain,
> to receive power and wealth and wisdom
>   and strength
> and honor and glory and praise!
>   (5:12)

CHAPTER 11

Emblems from Israel's Pilgrimage

In Israel's pilgrimage we have a picture of the pillar of cloud and fire, the guide of the Hebrew pilgrims through the wilderness, as it led them through many a changing scene of trial and education. All this is a picture of our life as the Holy Spirit leads us through the wilderness by ways we have not known.

It was customary, as we learn from history, for ancient armies to be preceded by just such a signal as this. Alexander the Great was accustomed to send before his army vessels of fire that sent up pillars of smoke and lurid clouds that the army might see which way they were marching. We know this to be true of many of the ancient Egyptian armies. So it was natural for the Israelites, or rather it was beyond the natural, for it was not only suggested by men's customs, but also was infinitely higher and greater. The whole account of this divine figure is particularly sublime and instructive.

It is a little difficult for us to take in the picture. When they were on the march it appeared, probably, like an enormous cloud of smoke, visible to all in the pathway, and moving on with majestic form like some heavenly being guiding their path. When the camp was to halt, the movement would cease. And, instead of becoming a leader in their march it would spread like a curtain over the camp, becoming a heavenly pavilion sheltering them from the desert sun and seeming to spread the wings of the very motherhood of God about them, making them feel as though they were hidden in the secret of His tent. What a beautiful spectacle it must have been when this began to droop, and then spreading abroad her brooding wings, shutting out the rays of the sun, and becoming better than the shade of the palm trees or even their desert tents. They knew they might sit down under its shadow and find the heat of the burning desert become suddenly as cool as a summer day overcast by the grateful clouds of heaven.

Again as the night came on and the march was weary and protracted day after day, and they feared they might lose their way, it became literally a light around and before them, affording the cheer and safety which light always brings. When they feared that enemies might be around them, or behind them, as indeed they were when the Egyptians pursued them, it went behind and stood like a rampart with the artillery and garrisons of heaven, looking terribly down on their foes with a fiery anger which forbade them to approach God's protected ones.

If you trace this figure through the Scriptures you will see that all the references we have made are warranted. He spread it above them like a cloudy covering to shade them from the heat of the day and to lead them in the darkness of the night.

Sometimes from the midst of the pillar would come the voice of God. Often we are told God spoke to Moses, and one time God spoke to the children of Israel out of the midst of the fiery cloud. It was the type of God's presence with His ancient people. In the New Testament, it was a symbol of His presence through the Holy Spirit, the Lord Jesus Christ with His Church and in the hearts of His children. Thus this precious third person of the Trinity ever becomes the Guide and Guardian of our pilgrim life, and our hearts are turned to Him with gratitude and holy confidence. May that blessed Teacher fold us in the shadow of His presence that we may know by living experience what all this means. Oh, that we will not have to wonder about it, but each can say, "I know it for myself as well as the preacher does."

As a dear old lady said one night in one of our meetings: "I can't keep still. He is singing in my heart!" Standing there, apparently a foot higher than her ordinary stature, and her face shining like the glory of the ancient cloud, she said, "You don't need to tell me about that. I know it." It is the voice of the Shepherd. It is the wing of the mother dove. It is the presence of God. It is the Holy Comforter. It is that which has come to you. It is that which is in your heart. It is that of which He said: "The LORD your God is with you, he is mighty to save. He will take great delight in you, he will quiet you with his love, he will rejoice over you with singing" (Zephaniah 3:17).

A Supernatural Symbol

Let us draw a few lessons from this figure. It was a supernatural symbol. It did not depend on any of the laws of nature. It was not carved like a pillar of stone. It was not an embroidered banner, such as armies carry at their front. It was something not made by hands. It was a battle flag presented from the ranks of heaven and had no touch of earth about it. Indeed, it was contrary to the laws of nature. There it hung in the skies without any pole to support it. It walked in midair independent of the laws of gravitation. It was a supernatural token of the living God, who does not need to go by our rules and does not need to be dependent upon our ideas of things or our modes of working.

When the Spirit of God goes before you it is not always a presence regulated by natural laws. It is a presence that will sometimes overleap what you thought and intended. It was not an easy way for the children of Israel to go through the land of Arabia. And the way you are led may not be the way you would have gone. But it is not accomplished by your provisions or your precautions or your reasonings. If our lives are divine, their leadership will be divine, and our pathway divine. And we will frequently go where man would not dare to go alone, and where we would not expect to be sustained, were we judging by the light of our own reason or the principles of our own sense and judgment. It is a divine guidance, a supernatural presence, independent of all but God's own infinite power and will.

Light and Fire

Again, we see in this pillar of cloud and fire the mingled elements of light and fire, which have all their natural symbolic significance. First, there was light—the light of truth, the light of personal spiritual vision, the light of His presence, the light that shows us the truth and then the way that we are to walk. Himself the Light, Christ comes to bring us all our light and also the sight to see the light.

Again, the cloud as well as the light suggests something about God. Cloud is the opposite of light. The cloud hides the light, and the breaking of a cloud reveals the light. It suggests to us the idea of the shadow that hangs about His presence, the mysteries which we cannot always penetrate or perceive, and the fact that the leadings of the Holy Spirit are not always to be perfectly understood!

There is not only light, but there is veiled

light—light that comes to you in clouds and thick darkness, light that comes to you with its dark side as well as its bright side. Is it not true that He leads you by a way that you have not known? Is it not true that your life is hidden with Christ in God? That you will not always see what He means, and you will not always behold His unclouded face? When you look up for the light, lo! it is a cloud. Is there not a dark side to the Holy Spirit? Does He not sometimes hide you in the shadow? Does He not sometimes take you where it seems very dark? You asked God to show you joy. Instead of joy, it was deep humiliation and tears. And you did not know until afterwards that that was His blessed answer. But when you yielded and followed, the pillar of cloud became a star of light.

Not only is He represented as the light and the cloud, but the fire. Fire is more than light. The fire has warmth as well as light. Fire is the element of intrinsic purity and mighty power that gives us a sense of the living forces that are able to consume the evil, destroy the adversary and endue us with God's own might. God is a consuming fire as well as an illuminating presence. The Holy Spirit baptizes the willing heart with fire—a fire that consumes all that you would gladly lose, and quickens and purifies all the energies of the soul and clothes you with God's infinite power and righteousness.

Again, the pillar of old preceded them as their leader. So the Holy Spirit tells us we will be guided by His presence. The Christian that does not understand this is losing much that is most precious in his experience. God has told us He will go before us, that we will not be safe without Him, and that He will make us know His voice. Have you learned this blessed secret?

Again, the pillar of fire not only preceded them, but followed them. It went behind them and stood as a wall of terror and defiance to their foes. God is not only our Guide, but our Guardian. And we might rather have the Holy Spirit defend us than all the fortresses or bayonets of earth. This is His blessed word, "The God of Israel will be your rear guard" (Isaiah 52:12).

In ancient times the shepherds were accustomed to building a fire in the desert to keep the wild beasts away. So He says, "I myself will be a wall of fire around it . . . and I will be its glory within" (Zechariah 2:5). The fire may burn awhile, but Joseph comes out of prison at last. The tempter may triumph for a while, but David sits for fifty years on his throne and praises the Lord who has kept him so marvelously.

Those who trust Him will never be ashamed. Take the Holy Spirit for your Leader and your Defender. Leave your trials and your vindication to Him and He will take care of them—if you will leave them, utterly leave them there, and walk on in helplessness and obedience.

The Holy Spirit in Our Midst

This fire not only went before and behind them, but it went in the midst. We read that while they were passing through the Red Sea, the fire went through the camp, for a moment enveloping the whole company, and then taking its place behind.

This is the beautiful picture of how the Holy Spirit comes through our midst, not only walking before and behind us, but coming into our being, possessing every faculty of our nature and becoming the vital impulse of all our power.

It is beautiful to notice the time that He did this. It was not at the beginning, but in the very crisis of their lives, when they were going down into the dark floods pursued by foes from behind and about to take the hardest step they had ever taken. But at last a power they had not known came among them. It entered their hearts and bosoms, became one with their innermost lives. They could feel the conscious baptism on their whole being and they were not afraid. What a beautiful picture of the Holy Spirit in our lives! At first He is always ahead. We see Him as a doctrine. Oh, how that doctrine shines out when we first learn the truth about the Holy Spirit! When God first showed me this blessed reality of the third Person of the Trinity, it seemed I could never preach about anything else or pray about anything else. And I could scarcely feel patience with others because they did not always talk about it.

There was a time when this Blessed One seemed to stand as a great lurid light against your sky. You were looking at Him and following a little way off, as near perhaps as you dared. But there came a time when it grew so hard and dark. And then a voice said, "Go into this dark and angry flood. Step into the Red Sea." And as you stepped in you could hear the chariots of Pharaoh behind, and it seemed as though there were but a step between the soul and wreck. Then it was that the doctrine of the Holy Spirit seemed to disappear. And instead of that, in your very heart of hearts, the very depths of the soul, His presence came. The cloud moved from before and passed right through your being, and it has seemed to pervade and cover everything from that time—a conscious life that is part of all your existence.

Do you remember where the apostle says, "For we were all baptized by one Spirit into one body—whether Jews or Greeks, slave or free— and we were all given the one Spirit to drink" (1 Corinthians 12:13)? He baptizes you until you are buried as in an ocean, and then you begin to drink of that ocean until you are saturated with it. But it is in the hour of difficulty when all the resources fail, when even He cannot be an object for you to look at any longer, but must put His arms about you and take you closer. Oh, dear friend, have you ceased to look at the Holy Spirit, have you ceased to trust the Holy Spirit to do things for you and even to be your Guardian? Have you come to take Him in His indwelling, all-pervading life?—to see Him less and less and have Him more, and just partake of all the fullness of His life?

Again, this Holy Spirit was not only the Leader and Defender, the Baptizer and the Indweller, but He was also the Spirit of Rest. Many times He did not march, but stood still. Then He commanded them to stop and took them into the secret of His presence and bade them wait. And so with you, there will be times when you will not see your pillar. There will be times when Jesus will be in the back of the ship asleep. There will be times when you will be so empty, you will feel as though you never had anything in you, but you are an empty shell. There will be times when you will not have any place to go, or any of the restlessness of natural excitement. Ah, that is what tests some Christians so much. They get on well in the cavalry charge and when there is action, but to make them be still and wait on God, they fail. They break down. They cannot hear the voice which bids them rest. But in the pilgrimage of God's ancient people, we are told that when the pillar of cloud rested the people rested; at its going they went and at God's bidding rested.

The trouble with some of you is that you have gone before the pillar. There are a great many times when God wants us to keep still. A great deal of the Christian life consists in the little word of three letters, n-o-t. Read the Ten Commandments and almost everything in them is "You shall not." Read the story of the Christian life in that marvelous thirteenth chapter of First Corinthians, and you will find it full of the things that love does not do. So the greatest work of the

Holy Spirit is to call a halt and quiet His children and teach them to be dead to their own activity and work and plans. We must learn to allow the pillar of cloud and fire to rest, and then get quiet ourselves under His shadow from the heat of the day. So the Lord will be your Keeper and your Shade. Now the Lord is never your Shade unless you are still. When they were marching the pillar was not a shade. Every little while He saw they needed to be sheltered and rest a little. So He made them stop. If you are going to know the Lord as a Keeper, you will have to know Him as a Shade. Then it goes on to say: "The sun will not harm you by day, nor the moon by night" (Psalm 121:6); and then next comes: "The LORD will watch over your coming and going" (121:8). Ah, now you can march again. This beautiful psalm is the psalm of the pilgrim—the Lord leading and the Lord overshadowing you, without slumbering or sleeping, and so keeping you from this time forth, and even forever more.

The Glory of the Pillar

This pillar was most glorious at night. When the darkness fell and the lights of earth were gone, it loomed up there like a celestial palace in the sky or like the brilliance of the jasper throne. It hung over them in darkness by day, but only by night was it bright. And so you have found His presence brightest when every joy had fled. How the song just bursts out in the night, into loud hallelujahs. It was when the sun was set and a horror of great darkness fell on Abraham, that a burning lamp passed before him. It was when the disciples had climbed the rocky heights and it was the midnight hour, suddenly there shone a light above the brightness of the sun, and His garments became exceeding white, and a voice said, ". . . my Son, whom I love, with him I am well pleased" (Matthew 17:5). These are the hours of blessing. Oh, beloved! Turn them into transfiguration mounts with Jesus in the midst!

Again, this ancient pillar sometimes spoke to them. Out of it came the voice of God. So this is not a silent presence. "And his sheep follow him because they know his voice" (John 10:4).

Finally, it was a constant presence. He didn't take it away all through the wilderness. Even when they turned aside for a little time and it was withdrawn, He restored it again and said,

> My Presence will go with you, and I will give you rest. (Exodus 33:14)

> Neither the pillar of cloud by day nor the pillar of fire by night left its place. (13:22)

> He lifted them up and carried them all the days of old. (Isaiah 63:9)

> [He led them] in a barren and howling waste. He shielded [them] and cared for [them]. (Deuteronomy 32:10)

> Like cattle that go down to the plain, they
> were given rest by the Spirit of the LORD.
> This is how you guided your people to
> make for yourself a glorious name. (Isaiah
> 63:14)

Thus God ever led them. Even when they refused to go into the Land of Promise, after a little while He forgave them, and went with them through the wilderness, in the way He did not choose. And so this long-suffering Holy Spirit for two thousand years, nearly, has been treated by the Church of God as disobediently and yet He has not taken away for a day that illuminating presence. Through all Church history He is with His people and will be until Christ comes. He has been with you in your Christian life; even if not fully in you, He has been before you and behind you.

Only to the Jordan

This leads us to another thought. If not directly Scriptural, its lesson is at least most true. The pillar of cloud and fire led the children of Israel only to the Jordan. And when they entered the promised land with Joshua, it accompanied them no farther, but from that time forward the presence of God was veiled between the cherubim and behind the curtain of the Holy of Holies. Is there no teaching in that for us? May it not show that during the wilderness life the presence of the Holy Spirit is perhaps more marvelous, more wonderful, more startling? But when we get nearer to God, it is an inner presence not an outer. It is visible, not to the eye of sense, but in the chambers of the heart, even where we enter the Holy of Holies and dwell in the secret place of the Most High.

Have we not seen something like this in our own experience? At the beginning God led more by sense. There was more of that which the little child needs, object lessons, and bold pictures and scenes and a great deal of nursing. But when we got into the inner presence of God, when we had consecrated ourselves, utterly and unreservedly, when we had become His priests and kings and gone into the tabernacle of Jehovah to dwell in His pavilion, then the pillar of cloud was not seen in the sky, but His presence was more gloriously within, like the Shekinah presence in the ancient temple.

When you pushed aside the curtain and stood within the Holy of Holies, then you could see the glorious manifestation. It was not a cloud reaching up to heaven, but an ever-burning flame between the cherubim, where, until His people deserted Him in the days of Ezekiel, He revealed His glory not as the God of heaven riding on the clouds, but as the God who loves to dwell in the very secret chambers of the lowly spirit. Quiet, perhaps, and unknown to the world it may be, but it is a presence that fills the heart with constant rest and satisfaction. So, beloved, there is something better for you than even the visible presence. There is a place in your heart where He will come if you will take Him. If you will cross the Jordan and get out of the wilderness, if you will be willing to die in the floods that separate you from yourself and your past, if with Joshua for your leader you will pass in, and live by faith and not by sight, then you will find that inner place. Then you will find the Holy of Holies in your heart, where God will dwell with His own love and glory. Then you will know the meaning of such verses as this:

He who dwells in the shelter of the Most High will rest in the shadow of the Almighty. (Psalm 91:1)

If you remain in me and my words remain in you, ask whatever you wish, and it will be given you. (John 15:7)

If you make the Most High your dwelling— even the LORD, who is my refuge—then no harm will befall you, no disaster will come near your tent. (Psalm 91:9-10)

Yet for a little while I have been a sanctuary for them. (Ezekiel 11:16)

Each man will be like a shelter from the wind and a refuge from the storm, like streams of water in the desert and the shadow of a great rock in a thirsty land. (Isaiah 32:2)

Have you come into all this? Come this day into this inner chamber. Let the pillar of the cloud and fire come a little nearer. Let it descend from the clouds to the heart. Let not God be to you somebody way up there, but somebody right here, not somebody you see in the book or the vision, but a presence in your bosom, in your being—the Life of life, and Love of love.

Moses said, "If your Presence does not go with us, do not send us up from here. How will anyone know that you are pleased with me and with your people unless you go with us? What else will distinguish me and your people from all the other people on the face of the earth?" (Exodus 33:15-16). God had said, "I will send an angel. I will give the same power as though I were present" (see 32:33). "O, not so, my Lord, if your Presence does not go with us, do not send us up from here." And He said, "My Presence will go"; and that was not enough. "Lord, if You have heard my prayer in this, if I have found grace in Your sight, Lord, I beseech You to show me Your glory. Not only Your presence, but I want this Shekinah inside, this inner presence." And the Lord said, "Yes, you will see it. They can see the cloud, but come in, Moses, and I will hide you in the cleft of the rock, and I will make all My glory to pass before you" (see 33:17-23). And he came and revealed the name of the Lord, a Lord God merciful and gracious, keeping mercy for thousands. That was the inner revealing of God.

Dear friend, when He does come to you it will

be through faith. When Joshua passed over the Jordan his great promise was this: "I will give you every place where you set your foot" (Joshua 1:3). His was to be a life of faith. He believed in the unseen God, and God was revealed. Take Him today by faith, and so He will be revealed in you.

As I was leaving church one day, someone came and spoke to me. It was a woman to whom I had spoken before when her heart was very heavy and longing for His presence. I had asked the Lord to show her just what it meant. She came to me that day and said, "I have found it. The Lord came to me and said, 'Are You willing to trust Me by simple faith? Are you willing to receive Me with a heart that knows no joy, no sensible sign of My presence, and to trust Me without fear? Are you willing to be withered?' " She said, "Yes, Lord." And then she said all the terrors, all the darkness fled, and such tides of gladness just swept into her being.

So let us recognize that presence, even if we do not see it in the shining signal above us. It is hidden there. Don't you know that they of old could not always see the Shekinah? But it was always there. So trust Him. Follow Him. For that is the secret of His eternal leadership which God has given to those who obey Him. This is the secret, the joy of the Holy Spirit. The Lord help you to yield and rejoice in all the joy of the Holy Spirit.

CHAPTER 12

Emblems from the Wilderness (Part I)

When Pharaoh let the people go, God did not lead them on the road through the Philistine country, though that was shorter. For God said, "If they face war, they might change their minds and return to Egypt." So God led the people around by the desert road toward the Red Sea. The Israelites went up out of Egypt armed for battle. (Exodus 13:17-18)

Then Moses led Israel from the Red Sea and they went into the Desert of Shur. For three days they traveled in the desert without finding water. When they came to Marah, they could not drink its water because it was bitter. (That is why the place is called Marah.) So the people grumbled against Moses, saying, "What are we to drink?"

Then Moses cried out to the LORD, and the LORD showed him a piece of wood. He threw it into the water, and the water became sweet.

There the LORD made a decree and a law for them, and there he tested them. He said, "If you listen carefully to the voice of the LORD your God and do what is right in his eyes, if you pay attention to his commands and keep all his decrees, I will not bring on you any of the diseases I brought on the Egyptians, for I am the LORD who heals you."

Then they came to Elim, where there were twelve springs and seventy palm trees, and they camped there near the water. (15:22-27)

The wilderness journey provides us with many symbols and emblems of the Christian life. In this chapter we will study four and in chapter 13, we'll look at three more.

The Pathway of Trial

We have here a picture of the pathway through which God led His ancient people immediately after their redemption. It is symbolic, of course, of the pathway of our own pilgrimage, even as their redemption was the emblem of our redemption from the bondage of sin and misery.

We are told here that the Lord led them not by the way of the Philistines, which was near, but "around by the desert road toward the Red Sea." So we infer that God does not always lead us by the nearest way, and certainly not by the easiest way, as He calls us to Him. And this is the type of the trials of our Christian life. A reason is given:

"If they face war, they might change their minds and return to Egypt." God could not trust His people to go the easy way, and so He had to lead them the longer way to discipline them.

There are many other things about the way He led them which apply to us. The first was that He might have them apart with Himself and train them for the future. And so God has to take all His children apart to teach them. Jesus had to go apart into the wilderness forty days before He began His ministry. Let us not wonder if we share His life. Moses had to go forty years apart before God could use him. And Paul went three years into Arabia, where he was separated to God, and then came forth to do his Master's work.

When the gardeners in New York, the city where I live, are preparing their beds, they go out and find black loamy earth. Then they can raise almost anything in the ground that comes from the virgin soil. And so when God wants to raise spiritual harvest He says, "I am now going to allure her; I will lead her into the desert and speak tenderly to her. There I will give her back her vineyards" (Hosea 2:14-15), that is, from the soil that comes from her wilderness experience. So, beloved, if you had an easy path you would become a coward and run away every time you saw a Philistine. The people that have no trials and discipline are just like this; they are soft and cowardly. The one that God wants to make strong to undergo the journey to Canaan, He has to make hardy by discipline and training. He

leads you by the hard way that you may be har-
nessed, may be trained as a soldier to fight the
battles of your life, educated for your work by the
very things you are going through now.

Another reason He led them through the
wilderness was to show them what worthless
creatures they were. In Deuteronomy He tells
them, "Remember how the LORD your God led
you all the way in the desert these forty years, to
humble you and to test you in order to know
what was in your heart, whether or not you would
keep his commands" (8:2). That was another
reason why He led them through the wilderness.
If they had gone the short way, they would have
gone in with floating banners and the idea that
they were a wonderful people. But when God led
them this way, they soon discovered themselves.
They would have found it out later, when they
came into Canaan, and would have been defeated
by it. But God had to show it by the way of trial,
before they could come to their future inheritance.

And so God leads us through the wilderness to
show us what we are. There are people who can
go through a hard march all right, but when they
have to go through the hard little things, they
break down. They will bear severe pain or under-
take some great service, or seem marvelously useful in some public enterprise that gives them an
eclat of success and applause. Let them go
through a desert march, or where Sherman's
army had to cross the continent, or Napoleon's

army had to go through the Russian campaign, or Woolsey's army in Egypt, and they go through all right. But the little thing defeats them. They become sour and distrustful and ungrateful. If they do not go back to Egypt, they do not deserve any credit for it, for they would go if they could; and they blame Him bitterly because He brought them out.

Beloved, it is a wonderful thing to find out that God is not trying to show you how much you are, but how little good you can do by yourself. It was the most extraordinary discovery I ever made in my Christian life, when at last I found out that what the Lord wanted of me was to have a tremendous amount of failures until I broke completely down and gave up trying it myself and then had Him work it out for me. I had been looking to Him occasionally, but He wanted me just to depend upon Him all the time and to look to Him for everything. So He leads you through the wilderness. He wants to humble you, to prove you, and see if you will keep the commandments or not.

Another reason is to show how little this world is worth, how little it has that can supply an immortal soul, and how God can be the supply of the soul. He took them out into a barren wilderness where they had nothing to support the three million people a day. For all those years He supported them on the sands of Arabia, day by day spreading their table and making the water flow from the rocks, meeting their complaints and recriminations with blessing. They did not get their support from the desert. There was not any water there to supply them nor any bread to sustain them. Modern researchers have endeavored to explain the manner and method by natural laws. There are little plants in the desert. A few grains can be picked up under the tamarisk trees, a sort of balsam that drops from the branches sometimes; but it is not enough to support a single life for a day. It is ridiculous to try to explain the Bible this way.

The boundless and permanent supply shows that it was from the hand of God. This was intended to show that God can supply all our needs Himself. We read in Deuteronomy, "He humbled you, causing you to hunger and then feeding you with manna, which neither you nor your fathers had known" (8:3), that is, which is not a product of earth. He did this to show them that God was enough for their supply. This shows us that God leads us through the narrow places so that when everything fails us, He can do it for us. God leads some people through that kind of suffering so they can look the devil in the face and say, "God led me through this place, and nothing ever can be harder than the way He led me." He put Paul up as a sort of spectacle or exhibit. He said, "We have had all sorts of suffering; we have been sunk in the sea, and stoned until we have not a bit of vitality left." And then he says they were "sorrowful, yet always rejoicing" (2 Corinthians 6:10). God wanted to show that His grace was sufficient. When the desert affords no food, and all is a waste of desolation, then God will make it blossom as the rose.

Now, beloved, if God leads you through trying places, don't say, "it is because God wants to destroy me." It is that He may show you that He is able for that, and He can create a supply that would have never been known if you had not had that need. So turn your dark cloud into a background for a rainbow, and just begin to praise Him and rise through it to a deeper knowledge of His character. Will you take these lessons to yourself? It is the very way by which He is to educate you. How little you can depend upon your resolutions and plans, but He is enough for your trials and difficulties and even for the weakness and worthlessness of your poor, unreliable nature.

Now, let us look briefly at their trials and at the wonderful way in which God met them. The first was, no water. The second was, bitter water. And the third, threatening sickness. We are not told they had sickness, but the healing implies it. God led them into the wilderness of Shur, and they seemed to be threatened with a famine. Then they came to a fountain in the oasis. They went to drink, but turned from it in disgust, for it was foul and bitter. Then they turned in disappointment and anger upon Moses and upon God, and reproached them for having brought them on their journey. It is just like situations that come to us. We reach places where we seem to be shut in on every side. Perhaps some of you are there now. God wants to teach you that the old way is not to be the way any longer. You must look to Him and not to the springs of earth henceforth.

Then they came to water, and they said, "We have it at last." But it was bitter. Do you not know what that is? Do you not know what it is after you have turned to some old friend and leaned on some arm, to find, suddenly, that it becomes different from what it used to be? Your old friend does not understand you. And those things which you used to enjoy have no pleasure now. Perhaps the thing you look to becomes the opposite of what you sought. Perhaps the very thing that comes to you as a deliverer becomes the saddest trial of your life. God has to let it be so. Our first resource is to go to them. Instead of looking up, we have hunted in the desert to find springs, and found many. And God had to turn them into gall, and show us that the only real help could come from Him.

Then there came sickness, or threatened sickness. And so it has come to us. Oh, how God feels for poor, suffering men and women, especially those who carry heavy burdens under the strain of infirmity. How—as I have gone among the humble ones that toil for bread, as I look back upon what a pastor finds in the lives of those he lives among—how I have felt Christ must weep for the tired women that crowd our cities, that have the responsibilities of their children, and sometimes their support, and yet live such weary, suffering lives through physical disease. How I have thanked God when I have seen His help coming to these, and found that it can lift their burdens off their bodies as well as their souls. There is many a poor mother working all the day and half the night, carrying in her body some hidden disease. And it was upon such as these that Christ looked with compassion, because they were like sheep without a shepherd, and He healed them, and said to them in words that are not exhausted yet, "Come to me, all you who are weary and burdened, and I will give you rest" (Matthew 11:28).

The Branch of Healing

Let us now see the provisions of His grace for them. First, we have the sweetening of the bitter water. He let them find its bitterness, and then He turned it into sweetness. "So the people grumbled against Moses, saying, 'What are we to drink?' Then Moses cried out to the LORD, and the LORD showed him a piece of wood. He threw it into the water, and the water became sweet" (Exodus 15:24-25). The bitter waters were not taken away, but they were neutralized and turned into a source of nourishment. You know what this means. You know the difference between the sweet water that was always sweet and the bittersweet, more wholesome and more delightful to the taste of the mature Christian heart. That is what God does. He lets the bitter come, and when we have eaten the little book which was bitter in the mouth, in our inner being it is sweeter than honey. There are chastenings that seem hard and bitter, but afterwards they bear the peaceable fruits of righteousness.

Do you not know what it means to yield yourself to God so it seems a real death, to put your dearest on the altar and raise the hand to strike? And when it is done, oh, the blessedness of knowing that you pleased God, the ineffable sweetness of His words, "Now I know that you fear God, because you have not withheld from me your son, your only son" (Genesis 22:12). He seems to say, "I know what you feel. I understand you as no one else, and you understand Me as you never could have." Oh, the delight of being with Him in the dark places, alone with Him, and having His communications of love and grace, and saying, "You knew the anguish of my soul." And then, at last, you find the very things you thought the gates of death become the gates of heaven. The very thing you thought would break your heart turns your heart into songs of joy, and pathways open up that never could have come but for this obedience, this sacrifice of yourself to God's will.

How does this sweetness come? It comes by casting the branch of healing into the waters. And this branch is always at hand. God does not have to create it. It was growing by the spring. It is always growing near the trial, and you can always find the branch that will turn the sorrow into joy. How, sometimes, He has shown us a verse that we never saw before, and now our trial has turned into sweetness, and we have risen in victory and praise. How often when you have felt as though you must sink you have found a blessed promise and have cried out, "But thanks be to God! He gives us the victory!" Sometimes, when struggling with your wicked heart, He has given you a vision of His victory and with His coming the battle has ceased, and like the disciples you were at the land whither you went. We all have verses marked in our Bibles that bring back whole chapters of our life's history, and which we would not exchange for all the world.

You can go to London and read there on the towers, written by the fingers of martyrs and prisoners who have languished in the Tower, such promises. You can go to Rome and see them in the ancient catacombs, promises which enabled them to declare that the insults and torments of their persecutors were robbed of their sting just because the Lord Jesus Christ had made His Word real and had caused them to triumph over suffering.

Dear friend, have you learned to use the branch that grows beside your door, that turns your tears to joy?

The Covenant of Healing

We have not only this branch of healing, but the covenant of healing. "There the LORD made a decree and a law for them, and there he tested them. He said, 'If you listen carefully to the voice of the LORD your God and do what is right in his eyes, if you pay attention to his commands and keep all his decrees, I will not bring on you any of the diseases I brought on the Egyptians, for I am the LORD who heals you'" (Exodus 15:25-26). So not only did He provide for the trials of the wilderness, but for the physical infirmities of life.

Here we see first that this divine healing is to be from Him alone. "I will do it." It is to be a continuous thing. It is in the present tense. It is "I, the Lord your God, am healing." Day by day, He declares, "I will be the strength of your bodies."

Again, it is to be by obedience. "If you will listen carefully to the voice of the LORD your God and do what is right in his eyes." It is necessary that we both hear and obey. A great many of our sicknesses come because we are well-meaning, but we do not understand God. We go into the forbidden path without meaning to, and our diseases come again. So He bids us listen as well as do.

There is to be a distinction between you and the world. The Lord wants to put a line between the world and the Egyptians: "I will not bring on you any of the diseases I brought on the Egyptians."

We see further that this was a covenant and an ordinance for them. So this is just as much an appointment of God as redemption. And if you do not accept it, you are going to rob your life of one of its sweetest supports. We do not plead for any favorite idea, but we stand on God's ancient covenant, and God forbid that we should turn it aside. I do not see how any candid man can. The only way that anyone can try to explain this is by saying that this passage referred to the plagues of the Egyptians. But that would be ridiculous, because they had not feared any of the plagues of Egypt. They had not been subject to most of them. They had been kept from them, and now it would seem absurd for them to need this promise. Forty years later, God renewed the same promise and covenant again, in stronger words, "[I] will not inflict on you the horrible diseases you knew in Egypt, but [I] will inflict them on all who hate you" (Deuteronomy 7:15). And we know that He did not put the plagues of Egypt on their enemies then.

Notice another word in this ancient ordinance of healing. "There he tested them" (Exodus 15:25). It seems that this is to be a kind of test in our Christian lives, whether we will trust God or go to man. It seems sometimes as though God wants to show us whether we have a real trust in Him or are making believe because the things we trusted for are a long way off. He proved them to see how far they made God real. I have found, and I think many of you have found, that when sickness and suffering come, and you have to find whether you have a living God or not, it searches your soul. And when you have hold of Him, it makes God intensely practical thereafter in your life.

We do not want anybody to think that this principle of God's healing should be crowded upon any soul, or that you are to get into any bondage of conscience. God wants you to be fully persuaded in your own mind. But if you will take this ancient Scripture and trace your Bible through, you will find one uniform teaching—that God met His people with all-sufficiency for all their trials, and that He undertook to be for their bodies what He was for their souls—Jehovah Rophi, the God that changes not.

Dear friend, do take this into your lives. You that are struggling under infirmity and debility, how much you need this Christ to breathe into you His strength every moment! No words can tell how near it brings the Savior to your life to feel that every breath you draw is very part of His vital being. How sanctifying it is, how it makes you walk with Him in constant obedience, and how it seems to give you double strength. The strength that we get from Christ seems to go so much longer and farther. This supernatural strength is delightful. It almost seems as though one could not stop to sleep. It is not human. It is His. Every breath seems to accomplish more than mere earthly power. The things we do in this divine physical strength go farther. They reach the hearts of men; and God seems to set them going through eternity.

This is "a statute," a divine law, and you cannot experiment with it. You must take it with the certainty that it is just as solid as the Rock of Ages.

And if you take it, it will keep you until your life's work is done. It will not keep you forever. There will come a time when you can say, "I have finished my work." But until it comes, there is strength for you, according to all the measures of your needs.

The Wells and Palms of Elim

There is yet one more picture here—the wells and palms of Elim. They came just after the waters of Marah. "Then they came to Elim, where there were twelve springs and seventy palm trees, and they camped there near the water" (Exodus 15:27). This is a sweet break in the monotony of the picture—an oasis in the waste of desolation. It seems to rise before us with the soft verdure of loveliness and rest. As we read the passage it is like a very Eden of coolness and repose. The very name Elim speaks of rest and freshness. It is the type of the times of refreshing that God sends us after weary seasons of suffering trial. "Weeping may remain for a night, but rejoicing comes in the morning" (Psalm 30:5).

The wells tell us of supplies of water, and the palms of freshness in the midst of barrenness. There were twelve wells and seventy palm trees. I love to think of the twelve wells as standing one for every month, teaching that God has some new revelation of Himself, some new supply of grace for every changing season of life. And then the seventy palms tell us of a blessing for every year. Seventy years seem to be the average of human existence, and so there are seventy palms and twelve wells—a well for every month, a tree for every year. They tell us that all our life long we may be fruitful, and there is fruit to be borne in youth and also in old age. It does not mean that everybody ought to live for seventy years. But as that is God's measure of life, so God has as many palms as He has years. He has something for us to do at the beginning and something for the end.

Beloved, let us come to drink of these wells. Shall we call the first the heart of the blessed Jesus Himself? Surely, that is where we want to begin. And shall we call the second the blessed Comforter, the Holy Spirit, ever running over with joy and living water? Shall we find the third in the Father's everlasting and infinite love? Shall we find the fourth in this blessed Word of God with its endless supplies for every kind of need? Shall we say the next is the well of salvation, with water enough not only for our salvation, but for all the world's? Shall we call the next the well of grace, where we can come with our buckets every morning and fill them there? Then we have the well of holiness, the well of healing, the well of joy, bubbling over and ceaseless in its flow, the well of prayer where we can continually come and not find it too deep or say like the woman of Samaria, "you have nothing to draw with" (John 4:11).

Side by side with this stands the well of faith.

And, perhaps, best of all is that well which, like one of the geyser springs, is continually rising even above the level of the ground and sending forth new fountains on every side—we will call it the well of praise. So God bids us come and drink at all the wells. As the garden of God has its twelve manner of fruits, so we have these twelve fountains of blessing. We need never wonder at the freshness of His supplies of grace.

Some, again, apply this to the twelve tribes. It is blessed to think that there was a well for each one.

The seventy palms tell us of an infinite variety of fruits. The very fact that the palm tree grows in the desert shows that the Christian can grow anywhere. The palm wants the desert sun. It will not grow in the rich black soil. It wants the desert because it grows up and it grows down. It strikes its roots below the sand heap, and it sends its succulent leaves up, and if there is a breath of moisture, the palm tree can suck it in. And so God says that we are to be like palm trees in this, that we can grow in the hardest soil and find what we need in Him. If you have Christ in your heart you can grow anywhere. You can be a happy Christian in society and at home. You can be happy in uncongenial society, in the workshop, in the apartment building, or wherever you are. It is not true that we have to be ruined because our surroundings are evil. If you have the roots and the right kind of leaves, you can make the desert a garden. The people will encamp around you.

The palm tree has an infinite variety of fruit. They say they can make almost anything out of it. Out of the roots you get sago and arrowroot and many of the most delicious and valuable articles of commerce. The very fibers they weave into many useful objects. The sap yields delicious juices. Then we have the fruit, the date, coconut, and many others. The palm produces about a hundred staple articles of commerce. So if you are a palm tree, you will be good for everything— not only tall, stately, and nice to look at, but you will have a shade for the people around you, and you will have practical and substantial utility about your life. Moreover, like this ancient tree of Elim, you will keep growing and multiplying year after year, until in youth and old age you will have fulfilled all the ministry of a consistent and beautiful life, and it shall not have been one, but seventy palms.

But if we have the palm trees, we must have the wells. And if we have the palm trees and the wells, we must go by the way of Marah. We must start by the Red Sea and follow the pillar of cloud and fire. And we must not be afraid of the wilderness. Oh, will we not follow on hearkening to His Word till we will come to the waters of Elim and encamp there and sweetly sing.

> I've found a joy in sorrow,
>   A secret balm for pain,
> A beautiful tomorrow
>   Of sunshine after rain.

I've found a branch of healing
  Near every bitter spring;
A whispered promise stealing
  O'er every broken spring;
An Elim with its sunshine,
  Its foundations and its shade;
A handful of sweet manna
  When buds of promise fade.

Dear friend, God help you to turn into life this desert region. And I dare tell you in His name to follow Him. You will have the wilderness and the waters of Marah. But there is here a branch that will make it sweet. And oh, such blessed resting places by the way. And by and by, we will have, not Elim's palms merely, but the tree of life that is in the midst of the garden, and the water clear as crystal, and all the beauties of the paradise of God.

By and by there will be the river clear as crystal, flowing from the throne of God and of the Lamb, the tree of life with its twelve manner of fruits that yields its fruit every month, and the tabernacle of God with men, where the tents never will be folded, the encampment broken up, or the lonely desert ever return again. Happy day! All hail! Amen.

CHAPTER 13

Emblems from the Wilderness (Part II)

They all ate the same spiritual food and drank the same spiritual drink; for they drank from the spiritual rock that accompanied them, and that rock was Christ. (1 Corinthians 10:3-4)

No temptation has seized you except what is common to man. And God is faithful; he will not let you be tempted beyond what you can bear. But when you are tempted, he will also provide a way out so that you can stand up under it. (10:13)

These three verses give us the substance of three important incidents in the sixteenth and seventeenth chapters of the book of Exodus, describing the giving of the manna, the opening of the rock in Horeb, and the conflict of Israel with Amalek. These three things are all summed up in these three verses. "They all ate the same spiritual food," seems to be the manna. "And drank the same spiritual drink," leads us back to the rock and its flowing rivers. And the last verse quoted reminds us of the conflict and victory which they obtained in Rephidim as the type of our conflict and victory over our Amalek.

The Manna

The manna needs only a simple exposition, and the key to every exposition, I think, your own heart and experience must furnish. You will not understand this unless you know something of this hidden manna which Christ gives to him who overcomes. We read that some of this manna was put into a golden pot and laid up before the Lord to be kept for future generations. This teaches us that the real substance of this manna is kept for us through all the ages. For Jesus says, "To him who overcomes, I will give some of the hidden manna" (Revelation 2:17).

1. Supernatural Bread

The first thing we notice is that this was supernatural bread. It did not grow from the soil of the desert, but was somehow sent by the power and wisdom of God and given to them from above.

Likewise our spiritual life must be sustained from unnatural and supernatural causes. A Christian cannot subsist on his own strength. A Christian is more helpless than a worldling. The nearer you get to God, the more are dependent upon God and the less able to draw your life from the old sources. You will starve upon the husks of this world unless you have learned to feed upon this manna.

Are you living on the spiritual bread? Have you something in your life which is more than the breath of the oxygen and the carbon, which is more than the nitrogen of the food, and the phosphates and ingredients of bread? Is your soul feeding on something more than the thoughts of men and the affections and fellowships of life? Is your body upheld by something better than its own cohesive forces and elements? A poor lump of dust, how readily you fall to pieces. How you hunger and how you thirst, if you do not know something of this. Oh, you who have begun to follow Jesus, are you trying to live on the old comforts? You cannot do it. You must be constantly refreshed. You must be constantly comforted. You must be constantly fed from the love of God, from the thoughts of God, from the life of God. For He does not only give us His thoughts, He gives us His very heart's life.

2. *Simply Bread*

It was simply bread; there was no variety. They did not start with their different courses and various dishes and end with dessert. They had manna for the first course, and the second course, and the dessert. It was all manna, and they got tired of the sameness.

And so the Christian has only one kind of manna. That is the trouble today. They want variety. But God feeds His people on one kind of bread. It is Jesus Christ. It may be presented in a thousand forms, but it is Christ—a living Christ, a redeeming Christ, a faithful Christ, an overcoming Christ. The Christ in whom, and for whom you live. Jesus only. Are you satisfied, or are you getting sick of this one kind of Bread?

Did you ever notice that God said to the Hebrews that the reason He gave them this kind of bread was to prove them and see what kind of people they were? "Then the LORD said to Moses, 'I will rain down bread from heaven for you. The people are to go out each day and gather enough for that day. In this way I will test them and see whether they will follow my instructions' " (Exodus 16:4).

You can prove God's children by their tastes. If they love God and His Word, you can depend on them. He says again in Deuteronomy: "[He fed] you with manna, which neither you nor your fathers had known" (8:3). "He humbled you . . . to teach you" (8:3). Dear friend, if you have no taste for prayer and worship and the Word of God, you will be sure to break down. Your love for God's Word is a test of your spiritual character and faithfulness. You will never love God's Word until it fills you. You will never care for the Bible until it becomes bread to your heart.

A lady said to her friend, "I cannot like the Bible as you talk about liking it. It does not seem real to me as it seems to you."

Her friend replied, "The reason is, it never

speaks to you. Sometime when you are in trouble," and she was all broken down then, "you ask the Lord to lead you to some verse that He will speak to you particularly."

The next day her face was shining when she met her friend. She said, "Oh, He has given me this word." It promised her healing, and before the week was gone, she was indeed cured. Scores and scores of people have been helped by her simple testimony. When I saw her last I was met and welcomed by hundreds of Christians drawn together by her life and testimony. Six months before she had not any interest in the Bible, but she took the promise and lived upon it, and then she was interested.

God wants you to turn His Word into manna for yourself, and the manna is just Christ and His personal life.

3. *The Necessary Nutriment*

Although this manna only consisted of one kind of bread, it contained all that was necessary for the nutriment and support of their life. God just concentrated in that little round corianderlike seed all the elements of nutrition. Just as the chemists tell us that the milk we drink contains in it all the forms of nutriment necessary, so the manna included everything. How beautifully it teaches us that Jesus Christ is everything. I am so glad that you do not have to get Christ today, and then the next week hunt up some different gospel and some new sensation. But it is one thing, and that thing includes all others. "Just as you received Christ Jesus as Lord, continue to live in him" (Colossians 2:6). It is the same as when you first tasted it. It will be so through all the years to come. Jesus Christ will be the very same Jesus through all the ages of eternity.

Dear friend, do you believe that in that blessed Redeemer there are all the supplies of your life, for pardon, for sanctification, for wisdom, for redemption, for service? Do you believe that you can just take that personal Savior and He will become to you everything that you can ever need for comfort, victory, or for blessing to others?

4. *Insignificant Looking*

Again, this manna was a very insignificant looking thing, a thing that would be very easily overlooked. So Christ is a root out of a dry ground and despised of men. And this Bible is a very common looking thing in many houses, and many think it is a very dry Book. But only gather its manna and it will be, as we are told about this manna, as sweet as oil and honey.

This manna had to be gathered every day or it would become corrupt and breed worms. There are hearts, too, that are corrupting, and their very religion has mortified and turned to an open sepulcher because the people have not maintained their communion with God. They are living on the old manna of a century ago. The sweetest and purest truth will become infected and unclean if you do not constantly live on a present Christ and renew your communion every week and every day. You cannot live on the blessing of today, you must still drink afresh and feed on the Bread of Life, just as the Passover had to be eaten on that day and everything that remained burned with fire. You will learn that this daily abiding in Christ is the secret of your Christian life.

It is very beautiful that the manna fell on the dew. They found it in the morning imbedded or lying on the sparkling dew—a little grain of manna, a trembling drop of dew. You know the dew is the type of the Holy Spirit, the gentle Comforter that drops upon us His promises and His commandments, as if they fell fresh from heaven itself.

5. *Linked with the Sabbath*

Again, the manna and the Sabbath are strangely linked together. This chapter tells us about the Sabbath. For the first time since the creation we find it still observed. You know that a little more than a month later, the Sabbath was given in the Ten Commandments; but here before the commandment, we find the Sabbath existing. It seems as though God would show us that spiritual food and spiritual rest must go together. The Sabbath is the type of the peace that passes understanding. The people that are feeding on Christ are having Sabbath rest. Such people are not agitated by the troubles of life, but can stand the tempests of evil and trials of life and not be moved because their hearts are established in Christ.

Dear friend, have you learned the meaning of this? We read such strange and mighty words as these:

> I am the living bread that came down from heaven. If anyone eats of this bread, he will live forever. This bread is my flesh, which I will give for the life of the world. (John 6:51)

> . . . unless you eat the flesh of the Son of Man and drink his blood, you have no life in you. (6:53)

> Whoever eats my flesh and drinks my blood remains in me, and I in him. Just as the living Father sent me and I live because of the Father, so the one who feeds on me will live because of me. (6:56-57)

Do you know what that means? Jesus Christ, a living being, feeding your very being, as if a living soul were breathing life into you every moment, sustaining you inwardly and outwardly! Oh, may the Spirit reveal Him to you! This alone can satisfy and sanctify. This alone can make you strong for service. And this alone is Christianity. It is not the brain feeding on human thoughts or Christian doctrine. I say deliberately that all the Bible reveals is husks and not bread without this experience. One of the most distinguished of the

German commentators, who wrote on every book of the Bible, said, "I have written about them all. I have explained them all. I understand them in some sense, but I know nothing of it in my heart." That was not Living Bread; that was feeding on husks and on straw, but not on the kernels of His Word. Or that was feeding, if I might change the figure, on the raw wheat, and not on the flour. It is not the Bible only, or the Church only, but Christ making it all personal. There is the same difference between the letter with Christ in it and without, as between the letter I pick up on the street and know nothing about the writer and the letter I get from the friend I love. There is a person behind the latter. There is a Person behind this page. As you read it today, does it glow in your heart?

The Water

We turn to the second verse. "[They] drank the same spiritual drink; for they drank from the spiritual rock that accompanied them, and that rock was Christ" (1 Corinthians 10:4). The people had come to Rephidim, which was one of the oases in the Arabian desert, a place where ordinarily there were fountains. Indeed, travelers tell us today there are fountains there. It was a place of rest. They supposed they would find water as usual. But instead they found the stream dry, the trees withered, and everything desolate and barren. So the people burst out into wild clamors. They quarreled with Moses, and murmured against the Lord. They said, "Is the Lord among us or not?" (Exodus 17:7).

God, instead of meeting them with judgment as they deserved, met them as He ever did. He told Moses to call the elders aside. They were responsible men that could bear witness of it, as the disciples could afterward tell of the resurrection of Jesus. He took these men with him to the place of the fountain. There before the rock, the pillar of cloud and fire took its stand, towering above it. Moses took the rod and struck the rock, and instantly there poured from it a stream of water which spread through the camp and through the oasis, until the people, with eager cries of gladness, were struggling for it and drinking its flowing tides. Eastern travelers tell us what the caravans do when they come to water, they are so delighted. The horses plunge in, and the people crowd upon one another into the stream, until their cries of delight are mingled with shouts of alarm, as they trample each other in their eagerness.

So here the Israelites brought their suffering cattle and they all drank and drank. And it would seem that this fountain never closed, but the waters continued to pour forth until it became a living stream. For Paul says they "drank from the rock that accompanied them" (1 Corinthians 10:4). It went along as they went along. And though sometimes it could not be found above the ground, they could dig down and find it, they could open a little cavity, and it would burst forth again. So there was water all through the desert from this opening in the rock. They drank of the Rock that followed them, and it was the same spiritual Rock. It was Christ.

Water is one of the symbols of spiritual things. We see it in Genesis in the story of poor Hagar. We find its preciousness again in the reign of Ahab and the life of Elijah. Christ tells the woman of Samaria of the well of water springing up into everlasting life. John speaks of the river clear as crystal that flows from the throne of God and the Lamb, and to which the Spirit and the Bride say come, and of which all who will may take freely.

For us this means the fullness of salvation. More specifically it means the work of the Holy Spirit. The bread is the type of Jesus, and the water of the Holy Spirit. The Holy Spirit is referred to under this image of water in His refreshing grace. Flowing around us in the ocean, above us in the air, the moisture that fills the atmosphere, and without which life cannot exist, one of the most important ingredients that constitute the physical universe, water is the vivid symbol of His infinite and unlimited grace. It tells also of the freeness of the Holy Spirit for all who will receive Him without money and without price.

Notice, first, that this water comes from the riven rock. The rod of the lawgiver had to strike the rock before the water came. And God had to smite His Son before the day of Pentecost and the joy of the Holy Spirit could reach our hearts. Not only was the water started, but was left flowing, and ever since then the Holy Spirit has been in the Church. He is here today. He is for you today. There is no limitation of the fullness of His blessing to those who will receive.

Not only did the water continue to flow from the rock, but through the desert. A channel was prepared for it. When the channel was not there, it flowed beneath the ground. And so the Holy Spirit does not travel in aqueducts, but everywhere.

Traveling though Italy, I was struck by the vast aqueducts of the country, lifted up like our elevated tracks. If I had been thirsty I could not have reached them. God's water flows in all places. The great peculiarity of water is that it flows down. It will go as high as its fountainhead and as low as the neediest. And so the Holy Spirit goes through your desert life—into the hard places of your life, into your weary round of toil and down to the lowest depths of sin and misery.

I am glad that I know something of work, and Christ knows more. I do not believe that a lazy, indolent man can taste of the full joys of His grace. Christ walked the whole circle of our life Himself, and so these streams flow through your common life. Sometimes you have to pass through hours of trial, of toil and business, with all its pressure and its monotony. It does not matter much, if you have the divine supply and you can have it for the morning, and afternoon and evening, as well as in the hours of sacred service.

I do not know anything I am more thankful for than the sufficiency of Christ for the twelve hours of the day and the twelve hours of the night. I am sure I should have died long ago if I had not found in Him a continual refreshing and delight. I do not believe in merely getting through. I do not believe in riding in an emigrant train when I can have a palace car all the way. God will make it easy for you. He loves to see you put your hand on the hardest things and find them easy through Christ. This living water is for the desert, not for those glorious eminences. It will make your brain clearer and brush the cobwebs from your mind. It will help you who are toiling endlessly. How God's heart goes out to you. He knows what a life you are living. But He will go with you everywhere.

This is the sort of grace we want to tell the world about. We do not want a religion of silver slippers or kid gloves. But we want it to be practical heart work.

Conflict and Victory

The final lesson is the conflict with Amalek. I am so glad that God does not let the battle come until you have the bread and the water. If Amalek had come before the manna fell or before the rock was opened, I am afraid he would have had his own way. But God fortifies you for the battle by filling your life and heart with His sufficiency.

In the first place, this battle with Amalek stands

for the temptations that come to us from the flesh. Amalek was a descendant of Esau, and Esau was a man of the flesh. The whole race of Amalek includes the Canaanites. It stands for that in men and women which is animal. It stands not only for the coarse appetites of the animal, but also for the tastes and desires and ambitions which are fleshly, and not pure and heavenly. We can have a business that is earthly, and we can have a business that is consecrated. We can have joys that take hold on the earth, and yet are rooted in God, or we can have these things all center in the earth. Do you know what it is to have an earthly intellect as well as an earthly lust? Amalek stands for all this.

It seems Amalek came a long distance. He came unprovoked. He was not attacked by Israel; but he came himself, because he hated this new way, and he wanted to destroy it before they got to Sinai and the Tabernacle. Likewise, you do not know where the campaign will begin—perhaps on the way home, sitting at the dinner table, or in some of the things that will meet you before night. So Amalek came to fight with Israel. It seems to intimate here that Amalek will come till the end, because it says God will have war with Amalek from generation to generation.

Another thing I want you to notice—he came not where the pillar of fire was, but he came behind, in disguise, in strategy. We are told in Deuteronomy: "When you were weary and worn out, they met you on your journey and cut off all who were lagging behind; they had no fear of God" (25:18). It is so like his sneaking way. He came and fought the weary. If your face is set steadfastly to go to Jerusalem, he will not be there. If you are away in front, you will not see him. But if you are doubting and lingering behind and compromising with the world, afraid to trust God with all your heart, you will find him. He came and fought the hindmost. Don't get feeble. Don't linger behind. Do not take back seats in Christ's house. Always press forward. Where God promises anything, say, "That is for me." If God commands anything, say, "Lord, I will do it." When your faith or hope is weak, the flesh is apt to get control by its desires or its fears.

He is the type of our earthly adversaries that come in the world around us, and come often with combined and tremendous power. Oh, how easy it would be to prove this by turning back the leaves of your life. Dear young friend, what has blighted you? It is the flesh. What has sapped the springs of your life? Oh, if I could tell of the young men who come sometimes to tell me the stories of their downfall, it would make your heart ache. Perhaps it was unhallowed reading to gratify their fleshly taste, not very grossly at first—the book that pleases, the sensational columns of those devilish newspapers. It makes one sick all over to read the headlines.

That is where they begin, the lust of the flesh. But they go further. It has a strange fascination. Evil has a power to charm people. It throws such a glamour over them that they do not stop to think about the fearful depths to which they are descending. I would not venture to go into certain scenes of iniquity. One of the strongest Christian girls I know talked of visiting certain people. "I am going," she said, "to try to do them good." I told her of some lovely Christian people that went a while ago to convince certain people they were wrong, and were themselves lost. Another Christian woman went to hear Ingersoll [Robert Ingersoll, 19th Century agnostic] and she came to me a few nights afterwards and said, "He is the most glorious man I ever saw." The man had thrown over her the glamour of his intellect. It was a week before she recovered. My friend, avoid these earliest advances. It will come from behind, not in front. It comes in the theater, in the ballroom, every one of them saturated with the spirit of the flesh. And it gets more and more brutal and animal. As desire is gratified, it is harder to gratify it next time, and it goes on and on until the coarsest pleasures cannot satisfy its abominable thirst, and so it sinks, a rotten thing, to death and destruction.

So, dear friend, Amalek is the one that is destroying our people. A very authoritative voice was lifted up in one of the pulpits of this country in tones that ought to make one think, when it is necessary for one in such a place to speak such a warning. It is ruining the life of this generation as it did the cities of the plains. And even writing to the Ephesians and Colossians, the Apostle Paul, after he spoke of the heavenly places in Christ Jesus, warned them in the most solemn terms to abstain from fleshly lusts that war against the soul.

I want to tell you the remedy for this, as we learn it from this last verse. For all that may beset us, it tells us how to get deliverance from the flesh. You cannot deliver yourselves, that is certain. If Joshua had gone out alone to fight Amalek he would have been defeated. Joshua went and led the army, the same Joshua who led them into Canaan, the same Jesus, for Joshua and Jesus are the same—Joshua is the Old Testament Jesus. But while Joshua was leading the army, what was Moses doing? On the mountain with his rod, he was holding up his hand to heaven all the day long. And when the battle was finished, he built an altar and called the name of it Jehovah-nissi, "The LORD is my Banner" (Exodus 17:15). It just meant that he held up that hand and rod all day in token that God must fight the battle. Jesus leads us and God works upon the throne. So it is the Lord's battle and not mine.

A dear friend said to me in talking about this, "Do you not read in Exodus that God will have war with Amalek all the time? Haven't you and I got to fight this battle with self all the time?" I know there are thousands whose lives are embittered by the ceaseless struggle with their own thoughts. But I do not believe it is necessary. There are souls that have gotten above this battle. Israel had to fight with Amalek for forty years, and then God took the battle and Israel went in. I believe you can be delivered from this fight with the flesh. For we read that God will put out the remembrance of Amalek from under heaven. You will not need to be afraid all the time that you are going to commit some sin if you keep your eye on Jesus. I do not mean to say you are to be presumptuous, and are in no danger of falling. Any man is, unless he is abiding in Christ. So I said to this friend, "You don't read it right. It says 'the Lord will have war with Amalek.'" She said, "Is that what it means?" "Yes, it means the Lord will fight the battle with the flesh." "What a comfort," you may well say, and you may add, "Thanks be to God! He gives us the victory through our Lord Jesus Christ" (1 Corinthians 15:57).

Dear friend, the reason you don't get victory over the flesh is because you fight. Like the poor monk in the cell, you try to rub out the evil by penance and by suffering. But if you will just hand it over to the Lord, and take Jesus for your Leader, and lift up your hand and say Jehovah-nissi, you will find the passage true: "If you are led by the Spirit, you are not under law" (Galatians 5:18). God's almighty Spirit, not the strength of man or woman, will prove more than conqueror.

And then there is another thought: The Lord will have war with Amalek from generation to generation, and when an Amalek comes, the Lord will strike him down. Perhaps there is an Amalek in your heart that the Lord is having battle with. It is not you, but Amalek. The Lord loves you so well that He wants to slay the evil and set you free. When anything burns it is because it is not gold. It is tinder or stubble. When the Lord puts His hand upon it, it is because it is a thing that ought not to be there. So let us bring Amalek and all his seed to execution. If you find by your failures any place where he has power, bring him forward, as Samuel did Agag, into the presence of the Lord and slay him. While Saul was dealing gently with the captive king, reserving him for triumph, Samuel took a broadaxe, and cut him to pieces. Samuel was gentle and tender as a mother, but here was something that must be dealt with uncompromisingly. So if you have anything, bring it to the Lord and hand it over to Him.

There is another thought. "The LORD will be at war against the Amalekites from generation to generation" (Exodus 17:16). That is the reading of the text. But the marginal reading is: "Because the hand of Amalek is against the throne of the Lord." It seems to imply that this spirit of the flesh is rebellious and will not submit to God. There is no good in it. "The sinful mind is hostile to God" (Romans 8:7). It cannot be improved; it must be destroyed. The teaching is, you cannot make the old nature better, so you must give it to God.

There is still another reading in keeping with the construction, and it is very beautiful and striking: "Because Moses' hand (your hand, the

hand of faith) is on the throne of God, therefore
the Lord will have war." It seems to refer to the
hand of Moses being lifted up. It was grasping the
throne of God. It was Moses taking hold of Omnipotence. It was Moses not only asking, but
commanding, in the name of the Lord, and
Amalek was defeated by his authoritative and victorious name.

Dear friend, take this great thought with you. If
it is true, what a vantage ground it gives to faith!
You cannot only pray for divine help and mercy,
but you can rise up and sit down in heavenly
places, with Jesus Christ on the throne as king.
Put your hand on the jasper throne, as on that
lever that makes all the planets roll, all the suns
shine, and the kingdoms rise and fall. Put your
hand on the throne where Jesus reigns for you,
King of kings, and Lord of lords, and then you in
Jesus Christ can sit down at the right hand of
God, feeling that His hand is on the throne, and
if you are in Him, that your hand is on the throne
too. It is not only asking, but it is taking. It is not
only beseeching, but it is commanding in the
name of the Lord Jesus Christ. And when you are
thus delivered, and thus stand with Him in faith,
you will not fear the power of the flesh. You will
rise even above the world and the devil, and you
will understand what He means when He says: "I
have given you authority to trample on snakes
and scorpions and to overcome all the power of
the enemy; nothing will harm you" (Luke 10:19).

Surely this, whatever the reading, is the meaning: That this first adversary of Israel stands for the lowest, basest and meanest of our enemies— the one we fear most because it is hardest to fight with ourselves. It is an awful thing to have an inward insurrection, to have your being rent by the battle. "For what I want to do I do not do, but what I hate I do" (Romans 7:15). That is a living hell, beloved, and God does not want you there. But Christ will come into your heart and sit down upon the throne, and you will sit with Him on the throne, sweetly trusting Him to fight. Oh, beloved, when His love comes pouring in, the flesh will go out. It is dreadful to fight with some creatures, because they so defile you with their very touch. God does not want you to fight alone, but to have Him so in you and be so full of His life that the evil will be expelled.

I have illustrated it many times by the old figure, light the lamps and the darkness is gone. Bring in the light and darkness goes itself. There is the simple secret. Do not try to put out the darkness, let it alone. But bring in the light and God will do it. Keep your heart on Christ and Christ in your heart. "Live by the Spirit, and you will not gratify the desires of the sinful nature" (Galatians 5:16). Keep full of Jesus. Keep your tastes sweetened by His joy. Abide in Christ. Have Christ on the throne, and let the Lord fight your battles from generation to generation.

CHAPTER 14

Emblems from the Mount

You have not come to a mountain that can be touched and that is burning with fire; to darkness, gloom and storm; to a trumpet blast or to such a voice speaking words that those who heard it begged that no further word be spoken to them, because they could not bear what was commanded: "If even an animal touches the mountain, it must be stoned." The sight was so terrifying that Moses said, "I am trembling with fear."

But you have come to Mount Zion, to the heavenly Jerusalem, the city of the living God. You have come to thousands upon thousands of angels in joyful assembly, to the church of the firstborn, whose names are written in heaven. You have come to God, the judge of all men, to the spirits of righteous men made perfect, to Jesus the mediator of a new covenant, and to the sprinkled blood that speaks a better word than the blood of Abel.

See to it that you do not refuse him who

speaks. If they did not escape when they refused him who warned them on earth, how much less will we, if we turn away from him who warns us from heaven? At that time his voice shook the earth, but now he has promised, "Once more I will shake not only the earth but also the heavens." The words "once more" in-dicate the removing of what can be shaken—that is, created things—so that what cannot be shaken may remain.

Therefore, since we are receiving a kingdom that cannot be shaken, let us be thankful, and so worship God acceptably with reverence and awe, for our "God is a consuming fire." (Hebrews 12:18–29)

These beautiful words recall our thoughts to the mount of fire in the ancient wilderness, and they claim for us in the Christian dispensation all that was gracious and permanent in that awful and yet glorious manifestation of God, but leave out all that is dark, terrific and temporary.

In our review of the history of Israel, we have come at last to Sinai. We have followed them across the Red Sea and through the wilderness. We have seen them led by the pillar of cloud and fire, fed by the hands of God, refreshed by the streams from the desert, and made victorious over their enemies by the banner of God. But now the scene changes. I know nothing more vivid and impressive in their history than the strange alteration in the manifestation of God's presence at this time. Up to this point it has seemed as though a gentle mother had spread out her pinions and covered them with her feathers. But suddenly she becomes to them a form of terror. The voice that had been all gentleness and long-suffering and love, the God that had borne with them in their disobedience and frailty, seemed to change in a moment. As they looked at Him that morning, enthroned upon that fire-crowned mount, He was a living terror. The mountain was all in flame. It seemed to be rocking in a perpetual earthquake, quivering in the throes of dissolution, covered from top to bottom with the thickest darkness and smoke, while the lurid flames were flashing on every side. More terrific than all was the deafening roar of the trumpet; and, as it seemed, the mingling of the trumpets of a thousand angels was sounding on their ears and making their hearts to quake.

Even Moses, accustomed to seeing God's mightiest manifestations, called to his work from the burning bush and able to stay with God in the mount forty days, said, "I am trembling with fear" (Hebrews 12:21).

What was the meaning of this sudden change? What was the meaning of this hour? Up to that time He had met their murmurings with water and manna. But now, the message is:

> Cursed is everyone who does not continue to do everything written in the Book of the Law. (Galatians 3:10)

> You shall have no other gods before me.
> (Exodus 20:3)
>
> Be careful that you do not go up the moun-
> tain or touch the foot of it. Whoever
> touches the mountain will surely be put to
> death. (19:12)
>
> If even an animal touches the mountain, it
> must be stoned. (Hebrews 12:20)
>
> Even the priests, who approach the LORD,
> must consecrate themselves, or the LORD
> will break out against them. (Exodus 19:22)

Nor can the people hear His word. "Speak to us yourself," they cry, "but do not have God speak to us or we will die" (20:19).

Is not this a strange and awful change, as you contrast it with His gentle dealings with Abraham and Isaac and the children of Israel through the desert? What was the meaning of this sudden coming down to the mount and assembling them before the throne of His immaculate purity and inexorable law? There must be some deep sig-nificance for them, and for our lives. Yes, beloved! It was necessary that these lessons should be taught, and taught in this way. And it is necessary in your life and mine that the very same experience must come. It is the experience that comes to every soul that becomes thoroughly dis-ciplined and established in the life of holiness. I

believe this is the very picture of God's dealings
with many of us.

Out of Egypt

First, He took us out of Egypt, forgave our sins,
and led us through the wilderness with such a
gentle hand. We thought there never could be
any deeper experience. We thought the work of
our inner salvation was complete. We thought we
were so free from sin we should never know
temptation again.

As we now look back to our early experience
and see how free it was from temptation and
doubt, we wish that we could go back to the days
of childhood and return to that simple faith in
God. But there came a time when out of the
depths there arose the terrific forms of temptation that we never dreamed were there. As they
came, the face of God seemed darkened, and
there came the revelation of God in His majesty
and holiness, as He came to search the heart and
show us things we did not think were in us. Then
we became discouraged, and went to work to
make ourselves better. And when we sought to
rise in our own strength, we were knocked down
again by the hands of the law, and became so discouraged that we even doubted our conversion.

John Bunyan gives us a vivid picture of this. It
is after Christian has left the City of Destruction
and is on his road to the better land. Suddenly he
gets out of the way, and as he tries to get back he
meets with Moses, the man of stern face with no

ray of mercy in his countenance. Moses says, "Where have you been? What have you done?" And as Christian begins to tell his sin, Moses knocks him down. He cries for mercy, but Moses says he has no mercy, it is his business to give the law and to judge by the law. Christian rises again and is knocked down again. The lightnings gather on the mountain. He begins to despair when good Evangelist comes along and shows him the blessed way. And so he gets back again, but not by the hand of Moses.

So it was with us. Our disobedience terrified us. We felt ourselves weaker and more helpless than ever. God was only showing us His own face, and our hearts. He was showing us all this that He might lead us to something better than we had had before. He was showing us all this that we might get rid of the evil that was in ourselves, that we might get the strength of Christ in our hearts, that we might get the power of the Holy Spirit in our souls, that we might go forth to be saved not by our works, to be sanctified not by our attempts, but by the power of the Spirit of the living God, living and triumphing in our souls.

When we get past our Mount Sinai, we know ourselves better, and we know God better. I believe this was the object of God's revealing Himself on Mount Sinai. It was first, that they might see God. They did not know Him. I do not believe any man can know himself or be strong for true service, until he has seen something of the true majesty and glory of God, until upon his spirit there has fallen, not the vision, for men cannot see that in its fullness, but the revelation of God in His infinite purity.

So it was with Isaiah. He was not ready for his work until in the temple he beheld the vision of God's glory, and said, "Woe to me . . . my eyes have seen the King, the LORD Almighty" (Isaiah 6:5). So with Job when he cried: "My ears had heard of you but now my eyes have seen you. Therefore I despise myself and repent in dust and ashes" (Job 42:5-6). And so with Paul. His ideas were all confused and wrong until on the way to Damascus he saw Jesus, and was smitten and slain and altogether changed forevermore. There comes a time in a man's life when he gets the thought of God and sees his own egotism and pride and self-will. God lets him see himself, and then He reveals Himself, and God and His will henceforth are all, and the opinion of everybody else is insignificant. So it was necessary that they should see Him who was invisible, and that that mighty face should cover all the sky and blot out everything else.

His Holiness

Not only must we see God, not only must we see Him in His holiness, not only must we see Him as a consuming fire, but we must see Him as the God of love. I do not believe we can ever appreciate the love of God until we have had back of it the vision of His majestic holiness. When your very soul quivers in the fire of His purity, and you say, "how can I stand in such a presence?" Jesus comes and fills you and lets you come into that very purity. It is then that the love of God is so seen. It is when you have seen His justice and righteousness and His inexorable law, when you see that He will not accept anything less, that He will by no means clear the guilty, and that He hates sin with eternal hatred. It is then so blessed to know Him as your reconciled God, holy as Sinai, and yet satisfying for you every demand of His law through Christ who fulfills every requirement. It is blessed to look at His righteousness, justice and ineffable purity and think, "How will I ever attain to that?"; and then say, "Your holiness, oh Christ, is mine. Your purity You give me, Your very self You bestow on Your child, the cloud in which You are enshrouded, I wrap around myself, and in Your glory and purity, I come into God's presence."

I do not believe this glory ever seems the same to those who have not had the searching of His infinite purity.

Beloved, how has it come to you? Have you tried to make God a little easier with sin? Have you wished that God were just a little less rigid and would lower the standard? Or have you let the standard be the very highest and asked Christ to lift you up to it? God wants you to rejoice in His holiness. He does not want you to regret that He is so pure, but to remember that if there were any speck of sin allowed by Him in the universe, it would go to pieces in a moment. God does not save you by relaxing His purity one bit, but by bringing you up to it. He brings us to the heights of Sinai and enables us to stand amid its very fires in the robes of His own spotless righteousness.

So we read a little later that these people who were not permitted to come nearer, and who stood back because God was so holy, yet later could be received into His very presence. God said to Moses, "Come up to the LORD, you and Aaron, Nadab and Abihu, and seventy of the elders of Israel" (Exodus 24:1). And we see the very people that were not permitted to let the soles of their feet touch the base of Sinai ascending that hill, going higher and higher with Moses, where the sun was shining on them with all its cloudless glory, until the clouds were below them, and they entered within the very canopy of heaven. There was no lightning now, no stroke, no judgment. But they sat down on the mount, and God prepared a feast for them. And we read that "God did not raise his hand against these leaders of the Israelites; they saw God, and they ate and drank" (24:11).

They were visiting with God, and yet they were sinful men. They were in the very same mount which Moses and they had stood back from. What was the difference? Oh, this time when they went up, they had the blood on their hands. They had slain the sacrifice at the foot of the mount. They had sprinkled the blood over them. With this token they could draw near.

God was not any less holy; but that blood meant that full satisfaction had been rendered. It meant that they themselves, ceremonially at least, and as types of us spiritually, had been purified by the very life of Jesus, for the blood had been sprinkled upon them, and was the very type of the living blood of Christ. I wish you could understand the meaning of Christ's living blood. I wish you could see something more than the drops of death that sank down into the ground at Calvary. That was not all the blood. I thank God that He shows us that Christ has blood that is not dead. Christ has blood that is as full of life as that in your veins. That blood He will put in your heart. And when He puts it in your heart, you will have His life and His nature, and you can go into the very presence of God. It is not only that He died for you, but He lives in you today. And so we can come in where the Shekinah cloud is shining, and feel no spot of sin, without fear look into His face, and lean upon His breast, and hear Him say: "You are Mine. You are all fair, beloved. There is no spot in you." Why? Because the blood of Jesus Christ covers you, because the blood atones for your sins, and because the life of Christ fills your heart.

You sit down with God and eat, and drink, and see His face, and over you spreads the sapphire cloud of heaven and the banner of His love.

I am glad, beloved, that He is not less holy, but brings us into His very holiness to meet Him there.

Our Unholiness

Not only was that ancient mount designed to show them God's holiness, and the necessity of it, but to show them their utter unholiness. God never gave the Ten Commandments with the idea in His mind that men were going to keep them in their own strength. It seems a bold thing to say, but I say it reverently. God never gave the Ten Commandments with the understanding in His mind that men were able or willing to keep them, until they got something better than they had in their nature. He wanted them to be kept, but He knew men could not keep them until they had the Holy Spirit in their hearts, until they had the nature of Christ in their hearts. He gave them to show men what they could not do and how weak they were. Paul says that righteousness could not come by the law. He says that the law made nothing perfect. It was our schoolmaster to bring us to Christ. I do not mean that God intended them to break His law, but He knew they would, and when they said, "We will do everything the LORD has said" (19:8), God saw them in anticipation dancing around the golden calf, and He may have smiled when He heard that promise, and said, "Poor children, you do not know yourselves." And so He brings many a solemn test to let you know what you are. He holds up this standard of righteousness to show you how far you are from it.

This revelation of sin comes to every heart. We

see Job pleading his own righteousness and telling Eliphaz and all those miserable comforters he was as good as they were, and that it was almost a shame for God to treat him as He was treating him. And when he got through and had written his own autobiography, then God came in a moment, and said: "Job, look at yourself," and Job looked, and gave a great cry, and said: "I spoke of things I did not understand. . . . I despise myself and repent in dust and ashes" (Job 42:3, 6). Then Job saw his worthlessness and was ready for a better righteousness.

Dear friend, do you not know what you might do if God would let you? God had to let Peter down mainly to show him what Peter could do. He let Abraham tell a lie, that he might see that in the line of his very faith he was weakest. Paul says he, too, had a very happy time for a while. "I was alive without the law once. I thought I was good." Suddenly there came a great trial. I do not know what it was—something that touched Paul's pride. You know what it is when something comes and touches your pride. You say, "I will not," and God has to come and make you do it. "The commandment came and sin revived and I died"; that made him worse. The very moment he saw it was necessary to be done, he disliked it more than he had ever before. He found his heart was so weak and erring, he just gave a great gasp of despair, then he died, and God lifted him up to a better life in and through Christ.

I have not time to dwell on this thought. The

purpose of God dealing thus with us is to show us how wicked our hearts are and how much we need the power of the Holy Spirit in us, or we will certainly fail in the things we mean to do.

A Picture of Jesus

So, we come to the third lesson of the law. It has shown the people what God was, and how He would not lower His standard, and how wicked they were, and how sure to do wrong in their own strength. The next thing was that it should be a kind of panorama to hold up the pictures of Jesus and show them what He was. You know that from the moment the people broke the law, God went to work to show them that there was One coming who would keep the law—a Man, like themselves—and that glorious One would become the end of the law for righteousness. He would stand as their substitute and atone for their sins. He would bear the wrath of Sinai which they deserved. He would save them from the curse of the law, and having done that, would go to work and teach them to obey the law. He would put the law in their hearts and enable them to keep it. Nay, better than that, He would come down into their hearts and live there, and living there, would keep them. He would be their righteousness, their wisdom, their life.

He pardons me for having broken the law. Then He comes into me and enables me to keep the law. He not only does away with my mistake, but He says: "Now I will undo it. It is all pardoned. I have suffered. It is all settled. And now let us go on together and make it right. I will come into you Myself. I will put into you another Spirit. I will put My Spirit in you. I will write My law there. I will make you love it. I will put the desire there so it will be natural. I will make it spring in your breasts. This is the covenant I will make with you after these days."

"It will not be like the covenant
    I made with their forefathers . . .
because they broke my covenant,
    though I was a husband to them,"
        declares the LORD.
"This is the covenant I will make with
            the house of Israel
    after that time," declares the LORD.
"I will put my law in their minds
    and write it on their hearts.
I will be their God,
    and they will be my people."
        (Jeremiah 31:32-33)

I will give you a new heart and put a new spirit in you; I will remove from you your heart of stone and give you a heart of flesh. And I will put my Spirit in you and move you to follow my decrees and be careful to keep my laws. (Ezekiel 36:26-27)

So they got a new law. I am glad that Moses let the first Ten Commandments break. He let them fall out of his hands as he came from Sinai. He got discouraged when he saw the people and said there was no use in having a law. Well, I am glad it broke. God gave a better. He said in a few days: "Moses, come up again. I will give you another law. But I will not trust it to you to keep. I will put it in the ark of the covenant." And so after that, the law was in the ark. So Christ hides the law in His heart, and puts it in our hearts, so that the things that once we hated, we now love.

A dear friend said the other day that it seems as though there was someone else living in her. Someone seemed to be with her all night and praying in her heart even when she slept.

Oh, weary heart, there is something that will come in and be a living strength and victorious life. It is Christ dwelling within you. And so, in the New Testament, the anniversary of the giving of the law was turned into Pentecost. For on the anniversary of that very same day that the awful word came down from heaven, "You shall, and you shall not," on that very same day the Holy Spirit came down into men's hearts and said, "I will enable you to keep the law," for the Holy Spirit is our law. And so we read in the New Testament, "Through Christ Jesus the law of the Spirit of life set me free from the law of sin and death" (Romans 8:2).

Not only does He say, "I will put the law in your hearts," but He says, "I will be your God, and you will be My people."

We close with that triumphant picture,

> You have not come to a mountain that can be touched and that is burning with fire; to darkness, gloom and storm. . . .
>
> But you have come to Mount Zion, to the heavenly Jerusalem, the city of the living God. You have come to thousands upon thousands of angels in joyful assembly, to the church of the firstborn, whose names are written in heaven. You have come to God, the judge of all men, to the spirits of righteous men made perfect. (Hebrews 12:18, 22-23)

I do not know how near they are; but we are very near to them.

Let us add, "See to it that you do not refuse him who speaks" (12:25)—this mighty salvation, this mighty indwelling, inworking Christ. Receiving a kingdom that cannot be moved, a kingdom of grace and of power, let us have grace, not our own efforts, our own desperate struggles, but the grace whereby we may be enabled to serve God acceptably, with reverence and godly fear. He does not say, "Let us try our best," but "Let us have the grace of God to do it." And it will keep us, and enable us to so appropriate His holiness and love, that those words will not affright us, "our 'God is a consuming fire' " (12:29).

The gold is not afraid of the fire. The paper would be afraid, but the gold says, "Come on. I can come into your midst. You will not harm me." The paper burns, the gold grows brighter and ever burns on. Burn on then, celestial flame.

Refining fire, go through my heart,
   Illuminate my soul;
Scatter thy light through every part,
   And sanctify the whole.

CHAPTER 15

Emblems of
Grace in the Ancient Law

*So the law was put in charge to lead us to
Christ that we might be justified by faith.
Now that faith has come, we are no longer
under the supervision of the law. (Galatians
3:24-25)*

We looked in the last chapter at the dispensation of the law as it was especially significant and symbolic of God's spiritual order in dealing with His children under the gospel. We will now look at that which immediately followed the law—growing out of it like a flower growing out of the bosom of a glacier; namely, the types and symbols of the grace of God, so beautifully revealed to Moses by the Lord and through Moses to the people after the thick darkness and fire of Sinai had passed. There is no part of the Bible that has so many pictures of the grace of Jesus as this. It has been almost hidden by the thick clouds which are but the curtains of His glory, and behind which there are such visions of grace and beauty.

The law was our schoolmaster. Sit in the school and have the Master present the lessons. It was a kindergarten school, not an adult one. It was for the infancy of the Church, and so all its lessons are object lessons, and all its pictures are painted upon the canvas, or drawn upon the blackboard and interpreted by the New Testament writings.

Let us look at four of these object lessons of spiritual truth as they are given by God through Moses for His ancient people, but still more for our learning on whom the ends of the world have come.

The Altar of Earth

The first of these is at the foot of Sinai, before the smoke had cleared away, or the reverberation of the thunder had ceased to terrify the people. This first picture is very beautiful, but you might overlook it, it is so small. The wise have overlooked it. The moral have overlooked it. The deists and the rationalists have overlooked it. The poor sinner sees it, and how he rejoices after he finds it! How glad he is after that awful fire and tempest and that voice that says, "Cursed is everyone who does not continue to do everything written in the Book of the Law" (Galatians 3:10). How he rejoices as he looks at the base of the mount and there at its foot beholds this little object which I am going to show you, and which is so full of Jesus and His grace! Here in the very chapter that contains the Ten Commandments (Exodus 20:24) we find it. How different it is. The others are all, "Cursed is everyone who does not continue." This is, "I will bless." The other is, "You shall do." This is, "You shall sacrifice." The other is high above our reach, this is down low and everybody can get at it.

> "Make an altar of earth for me and sacrifice on it your burnt offerings and fellowship offerings, your sheep and goats and your cattle. Wherever I cause my name to be honored, I will come to you and bless you. If you make an altar of stones for me, do not build it with dressed stones, for you will defile it if you use a tool on it. And do not go up to my altar on steps, lest your nakedness be exposed on it." (20:24-26)

I suppose that you have overlooked that a thousand times. You have read the Ten Commandments and did not see this. You saw the awful law but did not see God's provision for the men that break it.

This is the first picture. The schoolmaster comes and touches the canvas with a few strokes, and you see this rude altar of common clay. If built of stone, it is to be the simplest stone. There were to be no graven tools used in its construction, no fingers cut on it as on our fine churches, and there were to be no steps. Some poor and feeble old sinner might come along and not be able to get up there.

It is the picture of the gospel. It tells them, in the first place, that Jesus Christ is going to come to this world to die for the men who are going to break this law. It is an altar where blood is flowing, where death is expiating sin by suffering, where the victim bleeds for the sinner. Then it is a place of great simplicity. It is the salvation that comes down for love of the sinner. It is the salvation that does not require him to carve it out with a chisel. Enough if he can heap a few stones together, and there offer the lamb of sacrifice that can take away his sins. He does not need to go up, or climb into a better state and make himself good. Anywhere and anyhow he may come just as he is and call upon Him that says, "And whoever comes to me I will never drive away" (John 6:37).

Thanks to the old schoolmaster for this beautiful picture. Beloved, do not forget its lessons for yourself and yours. As you meet the poor and lost, lead them gently to Him. They thought it would be an awful task to find Him. They thought they would have to work themselves to some higher place, that they had to fulfill the law ere they could be saved. But they have seen that Christ has died to take their sins away, and all they have to do is to come and take Him. Tell the lost and discouraged ones to build their altar anywhere and go at once to Him. You do not need a temple at Jerusalem. You can find it anywhere in your little room in the tenement house, anywhere that the poor sinner may be. No stairs to climb. "And whoever wishes, let him take the free gift of the water of life" (Revelation 22:17).

> The righteousness that is by faith says: "Do not say in your heart, 'Who will ascend into heaven?'" (that is, to bring Christ down) "or 'Who will descend into the deep?'" (that is, to bring Christ up from the dead). But what does it say? "The word is near you; it is in your mouth and in your heart," that is, the word of faith we are proclaiming: That if you confess with your mouth, "Jesus is Lord," and believe in your heart that God raised him from the dead, you will be saved. (Romans 10:6-9)

Beloved, are you a poor, guilty sinner? Have you known the law of God and broken it? Are you standing, conscious of your wrong, and hesitating what to do? Oh, you do not need to come as far as a church altar, but just where you are, you can lift your heart and say, "Oh, Lamb of God, I come."

The Hebrew Servant

The next picture is just as beautiful, but perhaps not so easily understood.

> If you buy a Hebrew servant, he is to serve you for six years. But in the seventh year, he shall go free, without paying any-

> thing. If he comes alone, he is to go free alone; but if he has a wife when he comes, she is to go with him. If his master gives him a wife and she bears him sons or daughters, the woman and her children shall belong to her master, and only the man shall go free.
>
> But if the servant declares, "I love my master and my wife and children, and do not want to go free," then his master must take him before the judges. He shall take him to the door or the doorpost and pierce his ear with an awl. Then he will be his servant for life. (Exodus 21:2-6)

That is, the servant is to be liberated and go, if he likes. He is a slave; but he is at liberty to claim his freedom. But here are his dear wife and children, whom he cannot leave without a breaking heart, for they belong to servitude by the conditions of their birth. He has his choice; he can stay with them and share their burdens or go out selfishly into liberty. He is a noble fellow. He says, "I do not want to leave them, and I will not." So the law provides that they can make a covenant. And he goes to his master and plainly says: "I love my master, my wife and my children; I will not go out free." Then he and his master go to the judges, and the master fastens the awl in his ear to show that he is bound over forever and is his voluntary slave. The understanding was that it was a willing servitude, and as such, he was honored.

This may seem to you a simple thing in the Hebrew code. But as we read the Bible, we see it again and again repeated as the type of the Lord Jesus Christ. Jesus, when coming to this world to suffer for you and me, uses this very language describing His coming. He says, "My ears you have pierced. . . . 'Here I am, I have come. . . . I desire to do your will, O my God; your law is within my heart' " (Psalm 40:6-8). You have nailed Me to the door. You have made Me a slave forever. You have made Me a slave of love.

You and I are called to be the Bride of Jesus, the very wife of the Lamb, for that is the picture of the Church in the Scriptures. We're poor slaves, bound over by our sins to a condition of bondage and servitude. Christ, the blessed Bridegroom, is free. Had He chosen, He could have stayed in heaven. He was under no obligation to come down and be bound under the law and endure the ignominy and suffering of the world. What would He do? Would He stay with His Father and the angels in that glorious kingdom? He said: "I love My wife and children. My ear You have pierced. I will take up the sins of the people. I will take up the tasks of the heavy laden. I will be the righteousness which they cannot provide. I will do for them what they cannot do. I will bear their burdens, and fulfill their obligations." So Jesus Christ was bound in the place of a servant for you and me. He says Himself, "The Son of Man did not come to be served, but to serve" (Mark 10:45). That is the reason why He was laden and crushed by our weight of sin, He was made a slave for us. He bought our liberty by the loss of His own. As the former picture was the picture of His sacrifice, so this picture is that of His righteousness, His obedience for us under the law, and His assuming for us all the burdens of our state of helplessness and sin.

Do you understand this for yourselves? Has this been real to you? You and I were under tremendous obligations; have we taken Christ for them? You and I were born under sin; have we taken Him as our Savior? We were heavy laden; have we let Him take our guilt? Have we thought what it meant to give up all for us? Let us say here to Him, "I love my Master; I will not go out free."

Let us be like the slave girl in New Orleans, when her master said, "Go, I have bought you."

She said, "No."

He said, "I bought you to set you free."

She said, "I will not go. I will be your slave, for you redeemed me."

So He became a slave for us that we might be willing servants for Him. It is easy to talk about it; but would you go for thirty-three years and drudge your life away for an enemy? Would you become a menial in the kitchen, a toiling slave of the brick field for someone that had never done anything to make you love them? He did it for you and me. He was tired for us. He endured the privations of life. He had no place to lay His head. He was driven from His childhood's home, about to be hurled over the precipice. And finally

He was hung on that cross outside the city for our sins. Shall we not say, "I love my Master, I do not want to be free from my Savior"?

He became a servant for me, I will serve Him with loyal love. Come, beloved, and let Him fasten you to the door, and the pain that pierces your hands and feet will be sweet. There will be a joy that selfishness never knew, as you look into His face and say, "I love You. Every drop of blood loves You. Every fiber of my flesh loves You. Every thought wants to be Yours." If you ever want to know a joy sublime, just say this from the bottom of your heart. I have said to troubled hearts, "Give yourselves to God"; and I have seen faces flash with glory, when they could say to Him, "I am Yours. I give myself unreservedly to You."

You know what the old English pillory was—a man nailed to a post by his ear. Christ was pilloried for you. Let us return His love.

The Vision and the Blood

The schoolmaster has given us two pictures. Here is another we will just refer to, for we spoke of it in the last chapter. It is the story of the blood. The altar tells us of the sacrifice, the servant, of Christ's righteousness and His service for us. And this third picture tells us of our access and our nearness to God, coming into the most intimate fellowship with Jesus.

> Then he sent young Israelite men, and they offered burnt offerings and sacrificed young

bulls as fellowship offerings to the LORD. Moses took half of the blood and put it in bowls, and the other half he sprinkled on the altar. . . .

Moses then took the blood, sprinkled it on the people and said, "This is the blood of the covenant that the LORD has made with you in accordance with all these words."

Moses and Aaron, Nadab and Abihu, and the seventy elders of Israel went up and saw the God of Israel. . . . But God did not raise his hand against these leaders of the Israelites; they saw God, and they ate and drank. (Exodus 24:5-11)

What a beautiful picture! It was the same mount that was smoking yesterday; but it is serene today, calm and heavenly, like the very gates of glory. Now Moses and these men were going up that awful mountain, and as they went there was no awful lightning or muttered warning of terror. They held basins of blood in their hands, and were all sprinkled with blood as they went. As they went out, the path got clear, looking like sapphire and as the body of heaven in its clearness. And as they reached some sequestered nook of the mountain, they paused, and behold, a table was spread. I do not know what was on the table, but it was the bread of heaven. The God of Israel was there. Perhaps it was the softened fire cloud of the Shekinah. There was something they knew to be the presence of God. They sat down around it, "But God did not raise his hand against these leaders of the Israelites; they saw God, and they ate and drank" (24:11). They looked up and it was as clear and blue as the sapphire of His palace. Their hearts must have thrilled as ours will when we sit down at the banquet of the Lamb.

It all meant that the curse was gone and that the blood had put away the sin, and that the blood sprinkled upon them was the very life of Jesus. They were the sons of God. They had been redeemed by the blood of Christ and could come as near as they liked. And we can have this blood sprinkled upon our hearts. His very life and nature is in us. We can come fully into the mount. We can eat and drink, and it will be the very gate of heaven.

Beloved, do you understand it? The first is the altar of sacrifice where He died. The second is the servant taking your task. And the third is the blessed Intercessor bringing you into the immediate presence of God—the blood shed and the blood sprinkled, bringing you nigh.

The exposition of it in the New Testament is this:

> Therefore, brothers, since we have confidence to enter the Most Holy Place by the blood of Jesus, by a new and living way opened for us through the curtain, that is, his body, and since we have a great priest

over the house of God, let us draw near to
God with a sincere heart in full assurance of
faith, having our hearts sprinkled to cleanse
us from a guilty conscience and having our
bodies washed with pure water. (Hebrews
10:19-22)

Beloved, are you living there? Have you come
thus near?

The Tabernacle

Again the wondrous schoolmaster changes the
scenery, and we look at the canvas and see on it
the picture of a little house of skins and boards, a
rude tent, but as we look within it is very beautiful. Outside it is just common boards and a few
rough badger skins for a roof, but inside it is all
glorious. It is hung with costly embroidered curtains of richest colors, and a flashing lining of
gold reflects the light from every side. Every ar-
ticle of furniture, even the simplest things in this
building are all magnificent.

We pass in, and as we come to the first opening we enter the court containing the altar of
sacrifice, and the laver, a basin full of water
where they washed. We come up to another
hanging curtain, we enter that, and are in the
building itself. On the left are the golden
lampstand and the table of bread. Before us a little altar from which incense and fragrance arise.
This is the tabernacle. And had we been permitted to look in once a year, we would have

seen another set of curtains drawn aside for a moment. We would have seen the splendidly robed person of the high priest go in, and as we looked in we would have caught a glimpse of the little ark containing some precious relics, and above it the cherubim, and between their wings a heavenly light which was the very eye of God. And that Shekinah arose above the tent until it became the pillar of cloud and fire.

This is the last picture that we will look at. It was the picture of the blessed Christ. It is the most instructive of all the types in the Bible.

I have told you that the other three pictures present Christ to us in different aspects—a sacrifice for sin, a provision for our righteousness, and our access to God. I think this last picture is the sweet thought of home. It is a house. The idea was that God was going to be the home of the children. He was going to make for them a home in this homeless wilderness. He was going to spread for them the Father's table wherever they were. Through that trackless, homeless desert with its loneliness, He was every night to pitch His tent and be to them a sanctuary and a rest wherever they were. I think it was of that Moses sang one day when they had been going on so long, and they had been dropping, dropping, dropping to bleach upon the sands as they passed, leaving their bones on the desert. He got so tired he said,

You turn men back to dust,

saying, "Return to dust,
　　O sons of men." . . .
You sweep men away in the sleep of death;
　　they are like the new grass of the
　　　　morning
All our days pass away under your wrath;
　　we finish our years with a moan.
　　(Psalm 90:3, 5, 9)

Then as he saw the tabernacle with its sweet refuge and rest for the weary, he thought of the God whose wings were spread over it, and whose bosom was within to shelter them, and he sang, "Lord, you have been our dwelling place throughout all generations" (90:1). Or, as it is in the more beautiful Hebrew, "Lord, thou hast been our home in all the generations." And I should not wonder if Moses wrote the next Psalm, it is so beautiful and fits so perfectly with the ninetieth Psalm. "He who dwells in the shelter of the Most High will rest in the shadow of the Almighty" (91:1). Yes, there is a home for you. We may, even here, dwell at home and sing, as we are going home,

　　Abide with me from morn till eve,
　　For without Thee I cannot live.

That home had three departments. First, the porch outside. In that porch there was provision for the guilty to put the uncleanness off their souls and off their garments. There was a fountain where they left their stains. But that was not home; that was only the porch. What a pity that so many Christians live in the porch. They do. Lots of Christians never get any farther in. They sit where the servants and the scullions are. A great many Christians come to Jesus to get their sins forgiven so that in some way they can go to heaven. But it is not the Father's house.

Drawing aside the next curtain, you go in where God's chosen servants always dwell. It was called the tabernacle. There was the golden lamp, and table of bread fresh every week, and the sweet altar of perfume, exquisite and homelike all the time. There they fed on God's bread and breathed the sweetness of heaven. It was where God's children banqueted on His love.

Some of you understand this. You know what it is to go in with Christ into the inner chamber and have a light shine on your heart that is not revealed to the world. To such, it is meat indeed and drink indeed. You are in the secret place of the Most High, dwelling under the shadow of the Almighty. That is what Christ meant when He said: "Remain in me, and I will remain in you" (John 15:4). Do not be so foolish as to dwell in the court. Suppose the prodigal had said, "Let me dwell in the kitchen; I do not want to go in there." That would have been an unworthy thing; and if he had appeared to be so unworthy that father's love would have been checked.

You are nothing in yourself, but Christ has provided the sacrifice, and He wants you to get the benefit. It would be a very foolish thing if you went to some great store in your city where someone had deposited a hundred dollars for you to use and said, "I don't feel free to take this. I will only take two dollars and seventy-five cents' worth," and go off. The merchant would say, "It will do me no good, you might as well have the good of it." And so, beloved, Christ has paid for the very luxuries of grace. He has paid for the best seats in His palace. Do not let Him feel that His fullness was wasted.

Then there was a third chamber beyond this, so glorious that they of the old dispensation could not go in, could not even look in. But when Jesus died on the cross the curtains of that inner chamber were rent asunder. When His heartstrings broke, there was a great rent opened, and they could see it open. The curtains burst asunder in a moment, and everyone could look in and see the Holy of Holies. Even heaven itself is now opened up to you and me, opened up so you can look in and not be afraid, so you can look in as He goes in before. You can look in and see your seat prepared and know that you will go in where the Forerunner has gone. You may not only look in, but you can live under its light and glory, making your pathway a little heaven as you go. Blessed, blessed home!

It tells us how the Christian is not merely a toiling servant, but a child at home. And it spreads its curtains for you when there is no other comfort and joy, and you can abide with Him until the time comes when it will be said,

"Now the dwelling of God is with men, and he will live with them. . . . God himself will be with them and be their God. He will wipe every tear from their eyes. There will be no more death or mourning or crying or pain for the old order of things has passed away."

He who was seated on the throne said, ". . . It is done. I am the Alpha and the Omega, the Beginning and the End. To him who is thirsty I will give to drink without cost from the spring of the water of life." (Revelation 21:3-6)

The Spirit and the bride say, "Come!" . . . Whoever is thirsty, let him come, and whoever wishes, let him take the free gift of the water of life. (22:17)

Come home, dear friends, come home to God's love, and stay at home. "Blessed are the homesick; for they shall find a home." There is one. Are you tired today? Is your soul lonesome? Is it weary? Come to Christ. He has got more than pardon. He can love you until you can feel it warm your heart, and know that it is not you, but He, that loves your love back again. Eye has not seen, nor have we dreamed what it will mean by and by. God be your home and give you the blessing of Him that dwells in the secret place of the Most High.

We bless God for the old schoolmaster. Lord,

it is good to be here on the mount; there is no man but Jesus here. The ministry of Moses is gone. "The law was put in charge to lead us to Christ" (Galatians 3:24). We have been looking at the pictures on the blackboard and while we have looked the Master has stepped in. He is here. O that we may go forth in His presence.

We will find it is not the Tabernacle now. It is a person. It is Jesus. And so we retire into the secret of our hearts, and say:

Blessed, gentle, holy Jesus,
    Precious Bridegroom of my heart,
In Thy secret, inner chamber,
    Come and whisper what Thou art.